BULLOCKS WILSHIRE

BULLOCKS WILSHIRE

MARGARET LESLIE DAVIS

BALCONY PRESS ✦ LOS ANGELES

For my parents, Catherine Davis and James H. Davis

CAST BRASS PLAQUE

Printed in United States of America by Navigator Press, Inc.

For information contact Balcony Press, 2690 Locksley Place, Los Angeles, California 90039.

Library of Congress Catalogue Card Number: 95-083656
ISBN NO: 0-9643119-4-1
10 9 8 7 6 5 4 3 2

CONTENTS

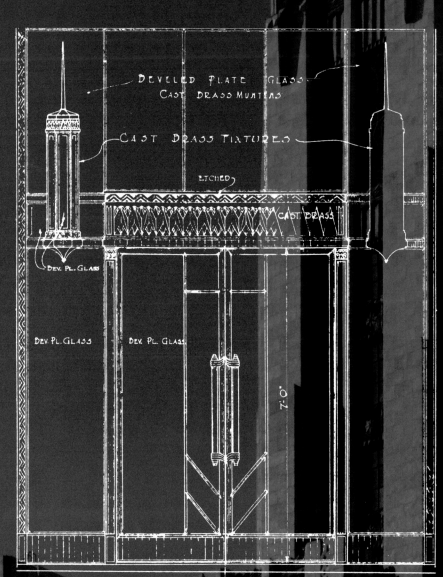

BEVELED PLATE GLASS
CAST BRASS MUNTINS

CAST BRASS FIXTURES

ETCHED

CAST BRASS

DEV. PL. GLASS

DEV. PL. GLASS   DEV. PL. GLASS

7'-0"

·ELEVATION·OF·ENTRANCE·N℃ 2·

THE DOORS OPEN

Tens of thousands of adoring visitors streamed through the doors of Bullock's Wilshire on Sept. 26, 1929, and beheld a modern department store so excitingly beautiful that it simply eclipsed everything else of its kind. An elaborate establishment that glistened in steel, terra cotta and copper, the structure was the first in Los Angeles in which art and commerce had merged into a new achievement of beauty.

Many of the curious who came that day were not merely shoppers eager to make their first purchases in the new store. They were there instead to pay their respects and offer congratulations on the achievement of the men who had made the store possible.

John G. Bullock, president of the company, and P.G. Winnett, its vice-president and general manager, were besieged with felicitations. Shaking hands, kissing women's cheeks and receiving well-wishers, the two partners circulated throughout, mindful of every detail around them. The families of both men stood in the background, present to witness the event and share the joyous tributes heaped upon the two merchant princes.

The praise, which had begun when the doors opened at nine o'clock in the morning, was followed by the serving of much fine champagne. Later that morning, architects John and Donald Parkinson, father and son,

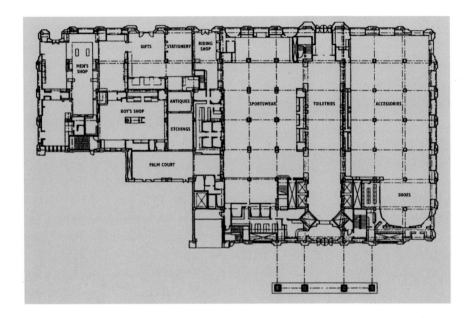

Left:
First floor plan, 1929.

Below:
Architectural detail of the Bullock's Wilshire storefront window.

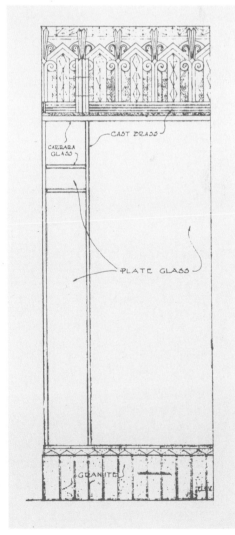

entered the store for their full share of appreciation and recognition for their originality in carrying out the spirit of Southern California in their design of the handsome building. The pair immediately was surrounded by a throng of supporters, who stood and applauded in a moment of great emotion. Scores of designers, decorators and artisans reaped accolades as well. Staff members attired in their finest suits and dresses were ready to tally the goods that caught customers' eyes.

The meshing of art and business was the result of hard work and industry — a stunning monument to the immaculate taste and vision of John Bullock. The beige-and-green edifice stood as a dignified and beautiful manifestation of all that Los Angeles could be.

The city celebrated the completion of the great emporium with near religious zeal. Possibly for the first time, contemporary art came into a home of its own in Los Angeles. In no previous attempt had there been so sympathetic an understanding and an outlay of so many millions of dollars to bring the spirit of modern art into a happy coordination with modern life as had been created at the Wilshire store.

"Bullock's Wilshire celebrated and climaxed the expansion of a decade," wrote historian Kevin Starr sixty-one years later. "Each feature and detail of the building bespoke the confidence and optimism of Los

Angeles in 1929: its sculpted mass rising ten stories from a base of five, reflective of the new City Hall downtown; the green copper siding against beige cast stone, as if the building were an oversized art object half encased in metal; the frosted glass and dark tropical wood of the interior; the disc and torch branch chandeliers ready to light an Art Deco Meistersinger with festival radiance."

A unique and extraordinary temple to the automobile, the grand entrance faced not Wilshire Boulevard but the rear parking lot, where expensive automobiles arrayed themselves in what Starr called "reverent formation like giant black mantises praying before a copper-green altar." The enormous store-front windows were designed to catch the eye of passing motorists. And inside, "to offer instruction as to what gods were being celebrated ... like icons in an Orthodox cathedral, were repeated depictions of the automobiles which had created a new type of American city."

When Bullock, holding his infant granddaughter, first opened the massive bronze-colored doors of Bullock's Wilshire that morning in 1929 and stepped inside the luminous central foyer of a "Contemporary Cathedral of Commerce," he presented to the city he adored a revolutionary concept.

"It is almost sacrilege to call it a store," wrote one critic. "It is a temple to many things, this new magnificent edifice erected by John G. Bullock out on Wilshire Boulevard at Westmoreland Avenue."

Framed in concrete and embellished in green metal and glass, the soaring lines of the exquisite Deco form with its tower crowned by a blue mercury light expressed "the spirit of America, bold, inquiring, aspiring."

Patrons arriving at Bullock's Wilshire drove through ornate bronze gates at the store's main entrance and entered the store's unique motor court.

DETAIL · OF · IRON · GATE

SCALE · 1½" = 1'-0"

THURSDAY, SEPTEMBER 26
AT NINE IN THE MORNING

BULLOCK'S

BROADWAY · HIL ... EVENTH

WILL PRESENT ... LOS ANGELES

BULLOCK'S WILSHIRE

ON WILSHIRE BOULEVARD
AT WESTMORELAND

BULLOCK'S WILSHIRE has been established in recognition of the growing needs of a great city. Introducing an era of the future in store design, it exhibits on every hand an attractiveness of personality, a difference and distinction that is a tribute to far-thinking vision, unremitting devotion and infinite attention to detail.

Bullock's Wilshire fits into its environment as an achievement of architecture and art—a Masterpiece.

Bullock's Wilshire will enter its epoch of life humbly—reflecting constantly the Inspiration of its Endowment—greeting Friendship with Sincerity—recognizing its responsibility to be the Perpetuation of Bullock Purpose "To build a Business that will never know completion" and that will strive always to secure "The Satisfaction of Every Customer."

Bullock's-Wilshire Motor Court with entrance from Wilshire Place—a service feature

"TO BUILD A BUSINESS THAT WILL NEVER KNOW COMPLETION"

John Bullock formally announced the unveiling of his grand new store in the Sept. 25, 1929 edition of the Los Angeles Record.

The streets surrounding Bullock's Wilshire were jammed for days with shoppers, well-wishers and the curious. In its first week, 100,000 guests had thronged to the great department store to be received by liveried attendants in the motor court and wander the marble basilica of the ornate perfumery, to ride the store's nickel, brass and copper elevators and to gaze at Herman Sachs' fresco-seco ceiling mural.

The seductive powers of Bullock's Wilshire caused critics and customers alike to find themselves spellbound by the dazzling interplay of color and light inside. Visitors moving from room to room found "an ever-changing, never-repeating succession of novel effects, a shifting, shimmering blend of suave color harmonies, of fabrics, of glass and metal and wood combined as if on a painter's palette."

From the daily newspapers to the most discerning architectural journals, rapture was the critical response. The collaboration of artists and craftsmen united with such potent, majestic force that visitors knew instantly they were in an extraordinary space. Few buildings ever have been built with as much effort to incorporate art into structure.

Everywhere the customer looked was a flourish. "Every detail, from drinking fountain to clock, ventilator grille, mirror hinge, has been evoked from the future and not from the past. Certainly the achievement is equal in magnitude to the designing of a great medieval cathedral," wrote one reviewer.

"Greece built temples. The middle ages built cathedrals. But we, whose life lies not in worship, but in producing and buying and selling, build great stores. The attainment in Bullock's Wilshire of a high degree of taste, of rightness, of soundness in thinking, strongly affects the quality and the taste of the merchandise shown, bought, consumed and assimilated into the culture of a city.

"With something like a click of recognition the newcomer entering the store is aware that he is not merely in a luxurious establishment cleverly planned in an authentic mode, but in the presence of a work of art."

In the years that followed, the legend of Bullock's Wilshire grew. From the "route boys" who rushed customers' purchases to the porte cochere to the maitre d' inside the popular fifth-floor Tea Room, Bullock's was home to a host of eclectic characters. Their pride and service defined the beloved store's golden age, when no present had more cachet than one gift-wrapped in a Bullock's bag.

Bullock's Wilshire became part of the fabric of Los Angeles, in the same category as a concert at the Hollywood Bowl, a dinner at Perino's or an evening at the Cocoanut Grove. It was the store where patrons shopped for wedding gowns, graduation suits and prom dresses. A place that reflected the best of Los Angeles' unique vitality and artistry, it was an architectural treasure that delighted the eyes of anyone who entered its massive bronze doors. Adored by the citizens of Los Angeles, Bullock's Wilshire and its grand days — its customers and their devotion, the movie stars, the rich and famous customers who shopped there and shaped the store's evolving role in the community — secured its place in the city's cultural soul.

*   *   *   *

Bullock's Wilshire's dramatic storefront windows were designed to capture the attention and imagination of drivers and passersby.

The store has been immortalized in both literature and film. Renowned mystery writer Raymond Chandler utilized Bullock's Wilshire and its soaring tower in his classic 1939 novel, The Big Sleep, in a scene that takes place at the east entrance to the store's parking lot when Marlow meets Agnes.

The motor of the gray Plymouth throbbed under her voice and the rain pounded above it. The violet light at the top of Bullock's green-tinged tower was far above us, serene and withdrawn from the dark, dripping city. Her black-gloved hand reached out and I put the bills in it. She bent over to count them under the dim light of the dash. A bag clicked open, clicked shut. She let a breath die on her lips.

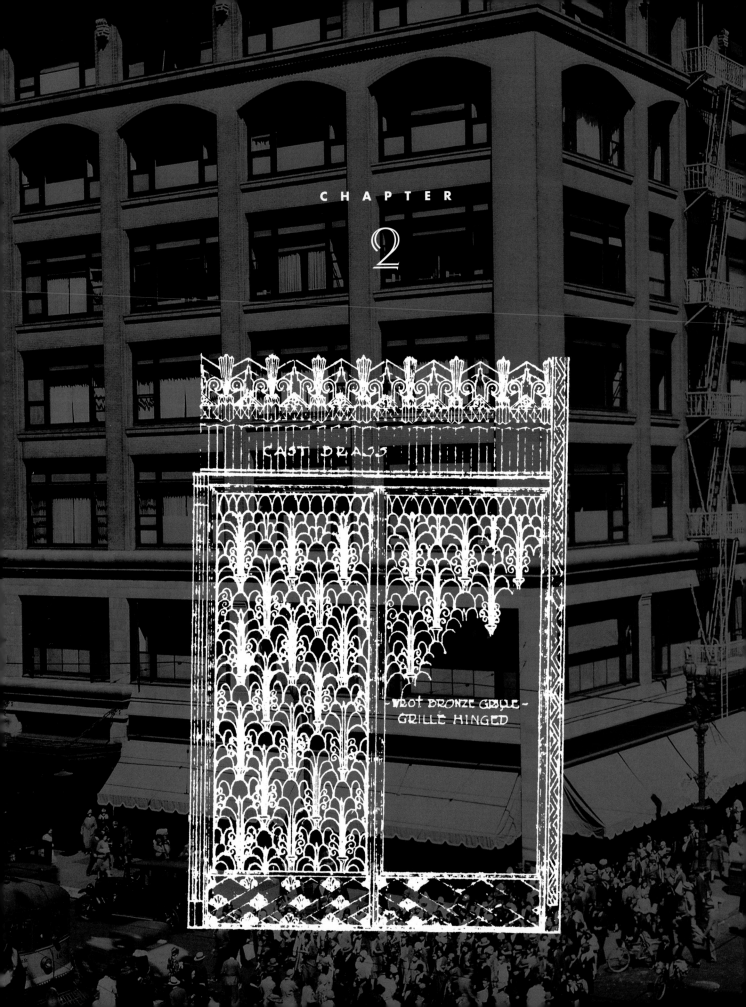

CHAPTER

2

THE ALTAR OF COMMERCE

"To the man of vision, business worries do not exist; they are merely problems to be met and solved."

— JOHN BULLOCK

John Bullock's dazzling Wilshire Boulevard store was widely heralded for its beauty and design, but the businessman who built it never lost sight of his primary objective — to move merchandise. The immediate success of Bullock's Wilshire was soon confirmed by the size of the crowds that surged around the building day and night following the store's grand opening.

"Every activity of the store should be directed toward efficient selling," Bullock said. "It pays to spend money for art in business when the expenditure follows this basic rule."

The man who would intuitively understand the proper balance of art and commerce was shaped by modest beginnings and a lifetime in the merchandising trade alongside two gifted men who were partners in Bullock's dream — his mentor, Arthur Letts, and his protégé, Percy Glen Winnett.

Born January 14, 1871, in the small town of Paris, Ontario, Bullock was the son of a hard-working Canadian railroad worker. His father died when Bullock was 2 years old. By the time he was 11, it was necessary for Bullock to find work to help support his family. He found employment at Munn & Co., a small local store. Young Bullock kept the shop open on Saturdays until midnight when his mother would fetch him to walk home because he was afraid of the dark. Bullock's pay was $2 a week.

Soon the entrepreneur was hired by Rheder's, the largest dry goods store in the vicinity. A defining moment came for Bullock when he was entrusted with a horse-drawn wagon to solicit and deliver orders. "It was my ambition while driving that delivery wagon to have some day, as big a store as Rheder's," he later said.

When he heard from his uncles about business opportunities in California, Bullock borrowed money for a ticket to travel to America. Bullock's intense longing to reach higher so impressed his mother that she gave Bullock $150 from her meager savings. His sister packed enough food for the journey, and Bullock set out for Los Angeles in January 1896. On his arrival, the 25-year-old Bullock deposited the entire $150 at Citizens National Bank.

Bullock frugally withdrew $1 or $2 dollars a week as he canvassed the city for employment. "My greatest ambition was to find work," he said. "I tried all over Los Angeles to secure such an opportunity. In fact, I tried every place, day after day, with that one idea — to get a job. At that time there were many unemployed and business conditions in general were very bad."

Above, left:
John G. Bullock — student and business partner of Arthur Letts — launched a retail enterprise that would make him one of America's great merchant princes. The Wilshire Boulevard store which bears his name was received as a "monument to progress" by the people of Los Angeles.

Above, center:
Louise A. Bullock married John Bullock in 1919. She was prominent in Los Angeles society and devoted much of her time to her husband's business and philanthropic interests.

Above, right:
Mr. and Mrs. John Bullock in formal wear at one of their many civic functions. Faultlessly groomed, Bullock and his wife helped promote the Bullock's mystique.

Facing page:
Pride and doggedness defined the complex personality of the enormously successful founder of The Broadway Department Store, Arthur Letts. Born in 1862 in Northamptonshire, England, he had $10 in his pocket when he landed in America. He is considered the founder and inspired genius of the colossal retail house that included both The Broadway and Bullock's.

In February 1896, while searching through a newspaper for work, Bullock read an advertisement that would reverse his troubled fortunes.

"I noticed that a bankrupt stock in a store on the corner of Fourth and Broadway was to be placed on sale the following day. Monday I was down at that store bright and early, to make my application. The man told me they had all the help they needed. I stayed around the outside until the store opened at eight o'clock, and then I continued to stay.

"The store was soon filled with customers and it was necessary to lock the front doors and not let any more in ... I went in through the rear door and the same man to whom I had talked was on the floor directing the work and doing everything possible to handle the business. He recognized me and said: 'Do you want to go to work now?' I replied that I did. He said: 'I will give you $2 a day;' and I was told to go behind the counter as a salesman ... "

The man who gave Bullock his first job inside the cramped 40-foot emporium was Arthur Letts, founder of the wildly successful, Los Angeles-based Broadway

Department Store. What John Wanamaker represented to the merchants of the eastern states, Letts represented in a similar manner in the Far West. He was recognized for his audaciousness in business and idealized for his marketing vision. During the next 10 years, Letts' downtown department store at the southwest corner of Fourth and Broadway would become a colossal retail house worth millions of dollars.

An emigrant from England, Letts had only ten dollars when he first landed in the United States. He arrived in Seattle in May 1889, where he secured a position with the retail firm of Taklos Singerman Company, and was placed in charge of the carpet department.

On Thursday, June 6, the whole 50-block business district of Seattle, the very heart and center of the city, was engulfed by fire. As the inferno approached the Singerman building, Letts and his fellow workers tried in vain to spare the structure. The firm's manager came to Letts and said somberly, "This morning, we were worth six hundred thousand dollars. In an hour it will all be gone. The flames will be here in 15 minutes. You may go now."

Twenty-seven-year-old Letts found himself out of work, miles away from home, with a wife and daughter scarcely 2 years old, and the city of Seattle lying in ashes at his feet. Letts doggedly decided to see it through and stay. He then realized that all of Seattle's stores had been destroyed in the calamity, yet the city's residents still needed supplies and apparel, and he reasoned that this might be an opportunity for him to start a store of his own.

Letts gathered a crude stock of goods and opened a men's furnishings store in a large tent. He painted his name over the entrance in letters so large that it was visible for miles. He slept inside the tent with a gun under his pillow so that no one would steal his merchandise, and more than once was awakened to see the canvas tent slit open with a knife. For months, the only time he went home was on Sunday mornings to be with his wife and daughter.

Letts attempted to open another dry goods business in Spokane Falls with the assistance of his brother-in-law but that venture failed miserably. In Seattle, things went from bad to worse, and Letts was barely able to survive and support his family. City authorities ordered that his tent had to come down, and traditional rents were too prohibitive for a man of Letts' modest means.

Letts stored his goods and attempted to fare better with the purchase of land in the small town of Seabeck, located in Kitsap County near the entrance to Darop Bay in Washington. By now, Letts' wife had given birth to a second daughter, and a son, named Arthur Letts Jr. Letts cleared several acres of land and built a log cabin, but the attempt at homesteading, was a failure.

After most of his savings were gone, Letts moved the family back to Seattle. Finally caught in the financial panic of 1893, he lost everything he owned, and not only left broke but was forced into indebtedness. He settled with his creditors at 35 cents on the dollar, and made a mental reservation that he would pay the debt some day in full. By now, Arthur Letts had spent ten years in the "Land of Promise," and all he had to show for it was bitter experience.

Arthur Letts as president of the National Retail Dry Goods Association in 1914.

Later, when Arthur Letts had reached the pinnacle of success, an interviewer asked him what he considered the real foundation of his accomplishments. "Failure!" he said sharply. "Failure put me through the college of hard knocks on the threshold of my business experience. It was tough at the time, but I can truly say that I owe everything to failure."

Letts became convinced that the only way he could prosper was to relocate to some city where the future held promise, and where he could start a business with limited capital and "grow up" with the city. He now turned his eyes toward the state of California, and the notion of the possibilities he could find in the city of Los Angeles fired his imagination.

When Arthur Letts arrived in Los Angeles, family in tow, it was a sprawling town of 60,000 people recover-

ing from the boom of 1887 and the panic of 1893. There was little outward indication of the great future the City of Angels might produce. Letts walked the streets day-in and day-out and observed the southward and westward trends of its business movement, where dwellings were being erected and businesses built in open fields. Letts had sufficient experience to know that the right location for his enterprise was fundamental, and that it had to be cheap.

One afternoon as he walked along Broadway, he came to Fourth Street, where there sat a little store on the corner that had closed. "The Broadway Department Store," read the sign over the window. To the average man, the intersection of Fourth and Broadway was "way out in the country," but Letts was convinced that it would become "the pivotal point of the city's retail trade."

On Feb. 24, 1896, at 7:30 in the morning, The Broadway Department Store opened for business with Arthur Letts as proprietor. It was a small, one-room emporium with a "heterogeneous collection of goods displayed upon roughly made shelves and counters — a little dry goods, some cheap candy, a few pots and pans, and a number of rocking horses, not so bright in color as they once had been."

Letts wasted no time in exhibiting one form of his ingenious sales strategies that would make him rich and famous beyond his expectations. Up to this time, nothing less than a nickel had passed for change in Los Angeles, and both merchants and customers never bothered with smaller change. Recognizing the "value of the unusual," Letts named the new store in his first newspaper advertisement and made a point of penny change: "The Broadway Department Store, the First to Use Pennies in Los Angeles."

The strategy proved sound, and customers went berserk for the chance to receive change in pennies. In

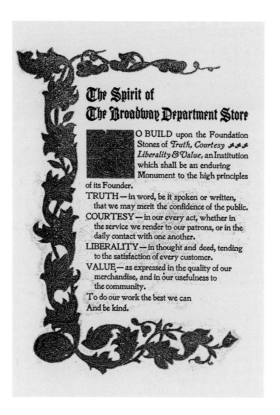

The Spirit of The Broadway Department Store

To BUILD upon the Foundation Stones of *Truth, Courtesy Liberality & Value*, an Institution which shall be an enduring Monument to the high principles of its Founder.

TRUTH — in word, be it spoken or written, that we may merit the confidence of the public.

COURTESY — in our every act, whether in the service we render to our patrons, or in the daily contact with one another.

LIBERALITY — in thought and deed, tending to the satisfaction of every customer.

VALUE — as expressed in the quality of our merchandise, and in our usefulness to the community.

To do our work the best we can And be kind.

later years, it became a custom at The Broadway to give away pennies as fitting souvenirs of the February 24 opening. Barrels of bright new pennies were obtained from the mint and one given to each customer after every transaction, no matter what the purchase.

It was into this store that John Bullock walked in 1893, just weeks after its grand opening, and he obtained his first full-time position from a harried Arthur Letts. The store became so congested with customers that Letts began work regularly at 6 a.m., and Bullock often was waiting for Letts when he unlocked the doors in the morning.

Within two or three days, Bullock had worked his way up to a position in the men's furnishings department. "No one placed me there," said Bullock. "I just seemed to drift that way."

The pressure was keen. Letts drove himself and others around him. He cut all corners and every hurdle was cleared to make way for success. Stock was piled on counters, empty boxes were strewn about the floor, the sidewalk was crammed with baskets full of merchandise.

At night, the cash on hand was counted and just enough "change" reserved for the next business day. Letts enthusiastically assumed the roles of buyer, advertiser, bookkeeper, window-dresser, sign-writer and general manager.

Bullock sold merchandise and selected new stock. Celluloid collars were flying out of the store at 3 1/3 cents each, and strenuous days of buying and selling did not cease. After the store was closed, Bullock often worked late into the night unpacking and pricing new goods, improvising displays and assisting Letts. Bullock's hard work did not go unnoticed.

One of the instrumental changes Letts instituted at The Broadway was the introduction of absolutely fixed prices. Initially introduced by Aristide Boucicaut of the great Parisian department store, Bon Marche, The Fair of Chicago was the first American department store to engage in the practice. John Wanamaker of Philadelphia and Eaton's of Canada also adopted the plan, but it had not been done in California. Letts carefully marked all the merchandise inside his store and forbid bargaining.

The practice made it possible for a child to buy in The Broadway Department Store, instead of the "shrewdest member of the family." All the child needed was the money and a description of the article required. If a customer was not satisfied with a purchase, he or she had the opportunity to receive an exchange check, good at any time for the amount of the purchase. Letts instituted the practice because he thought it was "fundamentally right." The merchant wisely counted not on casual sales, but on repeat business from satisfied customers. He wanted buyers to return to his store to trade and he knew they would come back if they had confidence that his prices were "fixed and reasonable." After he had worked at the Broadway for five months, Bullock was offered a half-interest in a baking business, the City Baking Company. Bullock told Letts he was going to try it. Letts said that he would like Bullock to stay on, and made it clear that he thought Bullock was making a mistake.

"I tried out the baking business for two or three days, getting up at three o'clock in the morning," Bullock said, "riding around the city in one of those baking wagons at break-neck speed, as the wagon used to go with horses, and after three mornings, I concluded that I did not care for the baking business."

Three days after Bullock had quit the bakery, a friend introduced him to the manager of a competing store and Bullock received a tempting offer to work at a salary of $15 a week. Bullock said he would think about it and he went to see Letts.

"Upon entering I met Mr. Letts, who said, 'Hello Bullock, do you want to go back to work?' "

"No, I don't know that I do."

"Well, I would like to have you back," said Letts.

"Well, I don't know. I have been offered $15 a week at another store." After considerable discussion, Letts said, "Well, Bullock, I can't pay you $15, but I might pay you $13 a week," and again stated, "Someday I hope to be able to pay you $75 a month."

The next day, Bullock returned to The Broadway and back to work for Letts. Bullock earned added responsibilities and rapidly advanced from menswear buyer to store superintendent. Soon Bullock was entrusted with engaging new help. Letts saw in Bullock the makings of a fine executive. Letts found Bullock a man endowed, above everything else, with character. "He was just, truthful, temperate, benevolent, magnanimous and sympathetic, and he passed that crucial test of genuine executive ability — he was direct and straight-forward with every man."

In 1889, just three years from the day it first opened, The Broadway Department Store was occupying the entire ground floor of the Hallett and Pirtle Building, as well as a building in the rear. The store continued branching out as the business grew. First one wall and then another was knocked down. Instead of 15 employees on the payroll, there were now 100. It was quickly apparent that Letts would have to obtain larger and more modern quarters. The hodge-podge emporium was no longer workable and Letts set his sights on property located at the intersection of Seventh Street and Broadway.

Meanwhile, Letts continued his vigorous sales campaign, and he made a year-long contract with the Los Angeles Herald for daily newspaper advertising. Letts' bold Broadway ads astonished and bewildered his competitors. Letts began with a bang and in his first month of business he spent one-third of the amount of money for advertising that he would spend for the entire year.

One such ad simply read, "On Wednesday, The Broadway Department Store will sell Douglas and Mean's $3.00 shoes for $1.50." And on another occasion Letts posted the following: "Notice. To whom it may concern: Any persons representing themselves as agents from The Broadway Department store are frauds, as we have no agents selling goods."

In this manner, Letts was sure that the public was never for a moment able to forget that The Broadway Department Store was doing big business at the corners of Fourth and Broadway in downtown Los Angeles.

At about this same time, Letts hired a 15-year-old Canadian named Percy Glen Winnett as a $2-a-week cashboy. Letts' selection of the enterprising teenager, who first came to work dressed in short pants, would prove to become an important influence in the lives of both Bullock and Letts.

Winnett, who liked to be called "P.G.," ran errands for the store and in his spare time was asked to string shoe buttons. It was immediately apparent to Letts that the adolescent did more work than he was supposed to, and Letts soon gave him the job of keeping up the sizes of the celluloid collars and other exacting tasks.

When Bullock was promoted to superintendent, Winnett, who was by then a clerk, took over as menswear buyer. Bullock and Winnett soon formed a fierce bond that would last a lifetime.

Arthur Letts talked about little except business, and he was remembered as never happy unless he was in the midst of action. Both Bullock and Winnett were fascinated by Letts' indefatigable efforts and business know-how, and the young men literally watched Letts build a million-dollar business from nothing but mental and spiritual capital.

For Letts, when an employee had risen to the level of department manager, that did not mean his efforts were confined to that department. "Do whatever there is to do," Letts often said. Department managers and store superintendents were expected to get to the store early, sweep it out and clean the sidewalks, and if necessary scrub the floors. Against all odds, and under Letts' considerable leadership and with the labors of hard-working Bullock and Winnett, among others, The Broadway Department Store took root, held its own and proved to be a phenomenal retail success.

In 1906, a group of men with plans to build an ambitious new store began construction of a seven-story building at the northwest corner of Seventh Street and Broadway. When one of the merchants died, completion of the venture stalled — with steelwork for the seven-story building having already been completed. Edwin T. Earl, publisher and editor of the Express newspaper, was left as the sole owner, and because he had much of his surplus capital in the investment, he found himself without a tenant and in a bind. Earl approached Letts, who decided that he might need the new building if he was unable to extend the lease at The

Broadway or if he needed to expand. Letts agreed to sign a 50-year lease with the stipulation that rent would be reduced during the first 10 years, during a "pioneering period."

Part of Letts' strategy was that this new interim store should be operated independently from Broadway, and he had a clear idea who he wanted to run it — 35-year-old John Bullock. Winnett was chosen as vice president and general manager. Bullock was instructed to organize a company and reserve that location in the event it should be needed for The Broadway Department Store.

Letts put up $250,000 to get the venture rolling, then stepped out of the way. Bullock resigned from Broadway on Nov. 1, 1906, and assumed full control of the new store, including hand-picking the merchandise and selecting employees. Bullock and Winnett set up offices in the Lankershim Hotel across the street from the construction site, where they hired a sales force of 400.

When it came time to name the new store, the pair decided on a short title. The men considered calling the new venture Bullock's Department Store, but Winnett argued for a shorter name, similar to the successful New York store known as Macy's. The new store was simply called "Bullock's."

Letts thought it was a good business strategy to keep the stores entirely separate, not only in accounting, but also in the eyes of the public. Few individuals were aware that the new Bullock's store was in fact owned by the man who had founded The Broadway. Bullock was given complete responsibility for the new enterprise. It spoke volumes for the confidence Letts now placed on the shoulders of his protégé that he authorized the business to be known as "Bullock's," while Letts provided all of the capital.

Bullock later had this to say about the man he considered his mentor: "To give you some idea of Arthur Letts' policy of giving a man a real opportunity and a chance to go ahead on his own initiative, I did not see or communicate with Mr. Letts in any way regarding Bullock's, until that Saturday afternoon, March 2, 1907 — four months later — when I called him on the telephone asking him if he would like to see the store, before it opened that evening at eight o'clock for a public reception. He came to the store at six o'clock as per arrangement, looked things over with his keen eye, and gave frank criticism."

The original Bullock's store opened with a lavish party reflecting the flair that would mark the team of Bullock and Winnett as talented taste marketers in the years ahead. Thousands crowded through the brightly lit building to listen to bands play on the lower floor and to see a pony show in the roof garden. "That night all roads led to Bullock's big electric signs," wrote Letts' biographer, William H.B. Kilner. "Thousands crowded into Broadway and intersecting streets, and it was a perfect jam for blocks in every direction. Men, women, children, women with babies in their arms, street cars, automobiles, and carriages, were all packed together, and at times it was impossible for either one or the other to move.

"The handsome, cream-colored building was ablaze with light throughout its seven stories, basement and roof garden. Standing high above the roof, the single word, "BULLOCK'S" could be seen from the outskirts of the city in every direction. The opening of Bullock's surpassed anything ever seen in the city."

When the store officially opened two days later, the few customers who braved a rare Los Angeles rainstorm found singing canaries and free violets for their patronage. Bullock's would give its customers violets every March 4 for years to come.

The handsome 157,824-square-foot building was designed by John and Donald Parkinson, a renowned Los Angeles architectural firm that would later design Letts' second Broadway Department Store at 401-403 South Broadway in 1915, and Bullock's Wilshire Boulevard store in 1929.

From the start, Bullock and Winnett strove to set their store apart by creating an aura of exclusivity, a

The rooftop garden of Bullock's downtown store soon after the gala 1907 opening. The single word "BULLOCK'S" ablaze with lights could be seen for miles in the Los Angeles skyline.

special personality that promised shoppers an experience they couldn't get elsewhere. The stock was of a higher grade and from unusual sources, the service solicitous and precise. Less expensive merchandise was found to move slower than higher quality wares, so the lower-end product was moved out in sales scheduled for August. After opening as a cash-only store, Bullock soon adjusted to meet upmarket expectations by establishing charge accounts, and Bullock personally designed an imposing coat of arms that read, *Suprema Regnat Qualitas* — "Quality Reigns Supreme."

As fine as the early years were, Bullock's was to face its first major crisis almost immediately. Six months after the store opened, much of the national economy was ravaged by recession following the failure of a New York bank. The merchants were further challenged by the fact that their new store was in what was considered a remote location at the time, off the familiar path of downtown's business district.

Bullock "was not shackled by fears and doubts," though it is hard to imagine he wasn't alarmed as business sharply dwindled in the recession. Empty cartons filled some shelves and the stock was spread thinly to cover others, but part of his strategy was to maintain an aura of success. Six of Bullock's delivery wagons, even though they were often empty and had nowhere to go, were driven around town as if business had never been better.

"There were days when 10 customers on the main floor marked unusual activity," wrote Kilner, "and many weeks when customers tendered paper scrip instead of money; days when the passing traffic dwindled almost to zero; a period when one whole floor was emptied because of lack of business and merchandise to fill it. Yet Bullock's never lost heart. Day by day they continued to gain the confidence of the public. They had established a policy, and nothing could persuade them to deviate from it."

The crisis may have been John Bullock's finest hour as a manager. He was enthusiastic and encouraging to his employees, who drew together and came to believe their store would ride out the storm. Contributing to high morale was Bullock's almost idealistic dedication to holding principle above gain. He demanded honesty in service and merchandise. He considered misrepresentation of anything inside the store an intolerable act of dishonesty. On his office wall was the motto: "The ideals of this business must not be sacrificed to gain."

Bullock himself paid close attention to customers, constantly alert to provide them an unexpected service or courtesy. Employees were expected to do the same, to hold promises as sacred obligations and ensure customers were satisfied regardless of cost. His premise was that cheerfulness, sincerity and courtesy would set Bullock's apart. It was to be a place where friendship was expressed through notable service.

Despite the Panic of 1907 and resulting recession, shoppers still bought into the Bullock's mystique. Two other large stores had opened about the same time: the Central Department Store and Bon Marche, but of the trio, only Bullock's survived. Bullock's revenues for the first year were a respectable $1.3 million. By spring 1908 the economy was beginning to recover and Bullock's was well-positioned to take advantage of it, grossing over $1.5 million for the year and turning a profit.

Letts had managed to secure a favorable new lease at The Broadway and by this time, Bullock's had advanced beyond expectations. Bullock's credit business now had over 1,000 solid accounts and was a proven success. Arthur Letts decided to maintain both stores independently on a permanent basis and one day he astounded Bullock and Winnett by announcing his decision "without prelude or preliminary."

Bullock and Winnett now put forth every ounce of endeavor to build Bullock's into a business without equal — one that would be widely recognized for its "courtesy, its sincerity, and its friendliness; to build a business that would be distinctive and different; to build a business that would be notable for its service; to build a business with one ultimate aim — the satisfaction of every customer."

The concept of providing customers with nothing but "the best" resulted in a business that grew so rapidly that in a few years, Bullock and Winnett needed to expand their operations. In 1912 a six-story building adjoining Bullock's was demolished and replaced with a new ten-story structure that almost doubled the size of the store. Five years later they expanded again by leasing an eight-story building on Hill Street and building a connecting bridge across St. Vincent's Court, a dead-end alley off Seventh Street. That gave Bullock's almost 400,000 square feet of floor space.

In 1919 the store expanded yet again and Bullock bought all the property from St. Vincent's Court on Seventh Street along Hill Street and connected it to the store. This provided Bullock's another eight-story building and more than 50,000 additional square feet. Bullock's was now the largest and most impressive retail venue in the West.

Next, Bullock desired to build another bridge across St. Vincent's Court in order to give the store unbroken frontage. He had encountered little trouble building the first overpass, but construction of the second turned out to be a far different story.

Only a handful of men in the retail trade were aware that Arthur Letts owned Bullock's. The public in general was unaware of the connection between The Broadway Department Store and Bullock's until the celebrated "Bullock's Bridge" controversy erupted onto the front page of Los Angeles newspapers in 1921.

John Bullock's commercial success earned him many friends in high places and one very notable enemy — newspaper magnate William Randolph Hearst. For reasons no longer known, Bullock refused to advertise in Hearst's Los Angeles Examiner and Los Angeles Evening Herald. The rival Los Angeles Times reported that this refusal provoked a spiteful vendetta by Hearst against Bullock. When Bullock commenced building the second bridge over St. Vincent's Court, Hearst mounted a full-scale campaign to thwart construction.

Bullock had been granted official city permits for construction of the bridges in 1917 and 1919. Work on the second bridge had already commenced when Hearst started his campaign against Bullock in 1921, and in January, the Examiner announced in a front-page headline, "City Makes Amazing Gift to Bullock's."

Hearst's newspaper accused Bullock of building in bad faith and demanded that Bullock pay the city rent of up to $80,000 a year for use of the space over St. Vincent's Place or be ordered to tear his bridges down. Bullock had already offered to pay rent, but the city attorney told the City Council no rent could be charged as Bullock had been awarded a proper construction permit.

A City Councilman in search of compromise suggested a private committee of appraisers for the Realty Board to determine the fair market value. The Examiner endorsed the plan until the appraisers came up with a suggested annual rental of $5,370 a year. Bullock promptly offered to donate that sum to the city annually, but Hearst was outraged by the low rate.

The "Taxpayers' Protective Association of Los Angeles" sent teams of youths paid by Hearst out on the streets to buy signatures at three cents each for a ballot initiative to revoke the permits and require rent of up to $80,000 a year.

The city attorney countered by pointing out a section of the city charter that would allow the city to accept a donation, whereupon Bullock offered to pay $12,000 a year as long as a connecting structure was maintained over St. Vincent's Place.

The proposed donation went on the ballot along with the Hearst-backed initiatives to revoke the bridge permits. Hearst called for the ouster of three City Councilmen who had backed Bullock and for re-election of the mayor who had opposed him. Hearst newspapers launched scathing attacks against Bullock in their news columns. The Herald called the councilmen who supported Bullock the "faithless five" and used derisive nicknames like "Cusser" Criswell and "Me-too" Sanborn. Hearst referred to Bullock and Letts as "purse-proud individuals [trying] to grab public assets from taxpayers already overburdened and underserved in police protection, street lighting and highway maintenance."

The Chamber of Commerce, the Merchants and Manufacturers Association and others banded together to fight under the slogan "Fair Play for Bullock's" and

Bullock's Wilshire looms in the distance in this eastbound shot of Wilshire Boulevard in the 1930s.

the Hearst initiatives were roundly defeated. The ordinance in favor of Bullock's was carried by a majority of six-to-one, and the two propositions were defeated almost three-to-one. The interests of John Bullock and Arthur Letts had been completely vindicated at the bar of public opinion.

By 1923, Bullock's was ready to grow again. A 10-story building was erected on vacant land next to the building on Hill Street acquired in 1917, and Bullock's was enlarged to a staggering 506,227 square feet. As the nation continued to prosper in the 1920s, so did Bullock's. Letts watched with pride as the reputation of both The Broadway and Bullock's grew to national pro-

portions and profits from both enterprises soared. The following year, Bullock's expanded twice more. The store added another 10-story building on Hill Street, and another block-long building was constructed for the delivery service, drapery and carpet workrooms, furniture repair and storage. Bullock's was now an imposing 739,156 square feet in size.

In the later years, Letts devoted much of his time to his investments in real estate and to his hobbies of horticulture, champion dog breeding and car collecting. His display of rare plants was considered one of the finest private collections in America, and Letts opened the sumptuous gardens of his Hollywood home to the public every Thursday. At his estate, Letts erected elaborate kennels for his beloved animals and imported from England the rare Ravenswood collies that he bred and exhibited. Letts' first automobile, the White Steamer, eventually gave way to a Tourist, followed by a Stoddard Dayton and then a Pierce Arrow. Finally, Letts succumbed to the luxury of a custom Rolls Royce.

Letts' first real estate ventures were in Hollywood, where he was a principal investor in H.J. Whitley's Los Angeles Pacific Boulevard and Development Company, which took options on thousands of acres throughout Hollywood. Letts bought up the land in front of his estate that lay between Franklin Avenue and Hollywood

Above:
All of Los Angeles mourned the passing of Arthur Letts in 1923.

Center:
Letts is laid to rest in a bronze casket smothered beneath a blanket of orchids.

Left:
The pulpit of St. Paul's Cathedral erected in memory of Arthur Letts by his children.

Boulevard, and opened it up as the Holmby Avenue tract. Letts built the immense Tudor-styled Holmby House with great care and precision, filled it with exquisite books and paintings, and encircled it by magnificent gardens.

The outstanding investment of Letts' career, outside the creation of The Broadway Department Store and the establishment of Bullock's, was the acquisition of the magnificent Wolfskill Ranch. The great ranch, encompassing 3,296 acres, skirted Pico Boulevard on the south for two miles and extended northward to the foothills three miles away, between the Los Angeles Country Club on the east and the Soldier's Home and a part of the town of Sawtelle on the west. It had long been coveted by speculators as the "prize of prizes" in local real estate, and it was with great pride that Letts purchased the vast acreage.

Letts entrusted subdivision of the great parcel to the Janss Investment Company. Part of the land between Wilshire Boulevard and Pico Boulevard was set aside for movie studio sites. On the adjacent land a new town-

site was planned to be called "Westwood." Not long after Letts had purchased Wolfskill, he conceived the idea that portions of the vast land would make a wonderful location for the University of California, and he directed 382 acres to be set aside for this civic purpose. The best parcels were subdivided into estates no smaller than three-quarters of an acre, and were named Holmby Hills in memory of Letts' British birthplace. The Westside Holmby Hills, as Arthur Letts had intended, achieved great fame for its residential charm and beauty.

In May 1923, Arthur Letts contracted pneumonia. In four swift days he was dead. Out of respect for his memory, John Bullock closed the doors to his great store. Hundreds of would-be customers approached and sought entrance, but after learning why the store had closed, "turned away with a shock as if it were a personal friend that had passed away."

The reach of Arthur Letts' fame and his many friendships was shown by the extraordinary number of cablegrams, telegrams, letters, and newspaper articles

Lifelong friend and business partner Percy Glen Winnett succeeded Bullock as president of Bullock's Inc. in 1933. Winnett guided the business through the Depression without an un profitable year, and orchestrated the profitable merger with I. Magnin's in 1944.

written on the occasion of his passing. Flags on all civic buildings in Los Angeles were placed at half-staff and fellow merchants paid homage in advertisements. From great associations and organizations, prominent citizens, mayors, governors and employees came messages of sorrow and condolence.

John Bullock and P.G. Winnett led the procession of mourners at the funeral of their mentor. The casket was submerged in flowers sent by the many who wished to honor his memory. The lid of the luxurious bronze casket was dropped into place, and the distinguished merchant prince was buried beneath a blanket of orchids.

Bullock was deeply struck by the sudden death of the man who had given him his first chance to work in Los Angeles and the opportunity to create a name for himself. Sadly, Letts did not live to see his former apprentice's most stunning financial achievement, which took place four years after Letts had passed.

Following his death, the federal government appraised the value of the estate Letts had left behind. They determined that the business of Bullock's, which Letts had launched just 16 years earlier with an original capital investment of $250,000, warranted a valuation of approximately $7 million. Among the other assets of Letts' considerable estate were his numerous life insurance policies. At the time of his death in 1923, he was carrying policies in 32 different insurance companies that totaled $1.8 million, all payable to his businesses.

In 1927, Bullock quietly formed a corporation called Bullock's Inc. to assume the interest held in Bullock's by the estate of Arthur Letts. The business community of Los Angeles was astonished when Bullock took the company public later that year.

In September, Bullock's announced the impending sale of $8.5 million worth of stocks and bonds. It was the biggest mercantile financing ever attempted in Los Angeles, and many believed Bullock was aiming too high. The following month, doubters were proven wrong. Four million dollars in Bullock's bonds went on the market and were grabbed up in less than an hour. Two days later, $4.5 million of Bullock's preferred stock sold in even less time. In less than two hours, $8.5 million of Bullock's securities had been sold, a remarkable achievement that was described in financial circles as "epochal."

The financial boon to Bullock was an outstanding expression of confidence on behalf of the public in both the man and his retail establishment, and Bullock's Inc. utilized the massive infusion of funds to expand yet again. In 1928, a building that occupied all the remaining space at Seventh and Hill streets was completed and opened.

Thus John Bullock, through the instruction and partnership of Arthur Letts and his association with P.G. Winnett, had launched a business that in six months was forced to weather one of the worst financial panics in American history — but went on to ultimately achieve renown as the finest dry-good store in the West.

It was a great accomplishment. "It was the vision and courage of Arthur Letts that made the enterprise possible," wrote Kilner. "It was the integrity and ability of John G. Bullock that carried it to success."

Putting into service what he had learned from the sagacity and industry of the master-merchant, John Bullock as trusted lieutenant set out to conquer an even greater enterprise. Soon plans were conceived for an even grander store of revolutionary character and beauty that would combine new concepts in art and commerce. It would be located along fashionable Wilshire Boulevard.

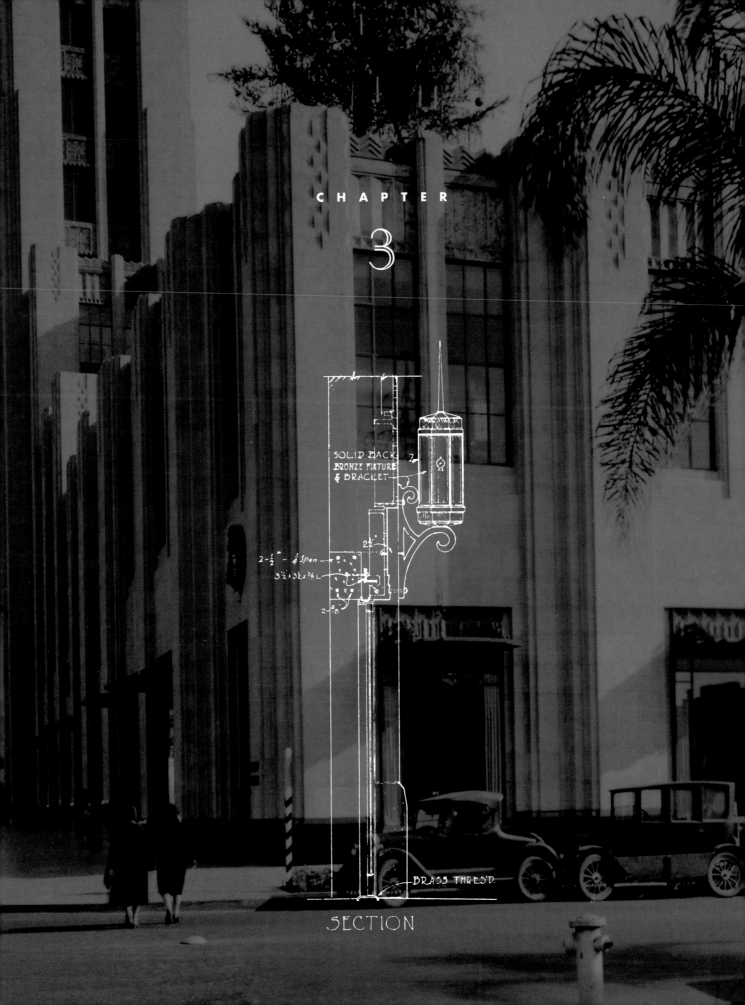

SOLID BACK
BRONZE FIXTURE
& BRACKET

2-½" – ¼ Span

3½ x 3½ x ¾ L

2-⅝"

BRASS THRES'D.

SECTION

VISION OF ARTISTRY

"Nowhere in all the world is there such a completely beautiful, aesthetic building as that which opens today on Wilshire Boulevard."

— ALMA WHITAKER,
LOS ANGELES TIMES, 1929

Wilshire Boulevard, the regal corridor of Los Angeles stretching from downtown to the ocean, was the vision of eccentric millionaire developer Henry Gaylord Wilshire, who pushed Los Angeles west along a street as wide and grand as his socialist dreams.

Described as "Fifth Avenue West," the boulevard that bears Wilshire's name became the fetching centerpiece for the city, eventually connecting downtown Los Angeles to the sea, a magnificent esplanade of handsome buildings and lush towering palms. The historic stretch of roadway became the playground of dignitaries and young starlets, millionaires and more.

The "Fabulous Boulevard" was home to some of Los Angeles' most revered architectural treasures, including the neoclassical Town House Hotel, the Ambassador Hotel and its famed Cocoanut Grove nightclub, the original Brown Derby restaurant, and later, the splendid I. Magnin department store and the swank Beverly Wilshire Hotel in Beverly Hills.

Affectionately called the "Champs Elysees of Los Angeles," Wilshire Boulevard by 1928 had become the city's most traveled corridor in the most motorized town on earth. By the end of the decade, the city's most elite businesses had begun to move there. Exhibiting the same keen business sense that they had seen under the

The "cathedral of commerce" dominates the skyline in the same manner as European cathedrals fancied by architect John Parkinson. It was quickly acclaimed "Los Angeles' most beautiful building."

direction of Arthur Letts, John Bullock and Percy Winnett responded to the city's passion for its automobiles and "Boulevard of Business" by selecting Wilshire Boulevard as the address for their new store location.

Bullock and Winnett astutely gambled that growth would continue west, and that the affluent suburbanites from the mansions of Adams Boulevard and the nouveau riche residents of tony Windsor Square and Hancock Park would pay top dollar to shop nearby. The two merchants acted on another visionary premise: that the carriage trade now owned expensive automobiles, and that customers would drive long distances to patronize a worthy destination. Shoppers were now expected to make the 12-mile trip to Bullock's Wilshire from as far away as Santa Monica, or the 17-mile trip from Pasadena at an average speed of 35 miles per hour.

Conventional wisdom held that a store outside of the central business core of the city could never draw enough customers to support itself and many businessmen believed the venture was doomed to failure. As Bullock's Inc.'s vice president, Winnett was credited with much of the behind-the-scenes efforts involved in the concept of building a full-sized store in what was then the suburbs.

In the early decades of the 20th century, Wilshire Boulevard, pushing west to Western Avenue, was the city's most fashionable residential district. Col. Harrison Gray Otis, editor of the Los Angeles Times, and Edwin T. Earl, editor of the Los Angeles Express, both built handsome mansions overlooking Westlake Park one and a half miles west of downtown. In the 1920s, United Artists president Joseph Schenck built the Talmadge Apartments for his wife, silent movie star Norma Talmadge, at Wilshire and Berendo Street. The

Van Nuys, O'Melveny and McCreas families built magnificent homes in Fremont Place, Windsor Square and Hancock Park.

Wilshire Boulevard had little commercial development, and Winnett's industrious efforts prompted the wags to call the Wilshire Boulevard plan "Winnett's Folly." The criticism served to make the feisty and diminutive retailer all the more determined to prove the naysayers wrong.

The proposed Bullock's Wilshire specialty store would be the first to recognize and cater to the emerging car culture of Los Angeles. Its main entrance would not be a grand portal on Wilshire Boulevard, but instead a spectacular porte cochere in the rear where motorists could make a graceful entrance away from street traffic. The store's automobile service would include liveried attendants who would park patrons' cars in a vast landscaped parking lot. Through the use of a "modern broadcasting device," attendants would ensure that a patron's packages were already tucked inside the customer's car upon his or her departure. The motor court and its focus on the automobile would be only one of many radical departures from established traditions in both art and business at Bullock's Wilshire.

THE ARCHITECTS

To design this flagship store that would focus on the automobile and incorporate new and exquisite elements of design, Bullock and Winnett selected one of Los Angeles' premier architectural firms. The father-and-son firm, Parkinson and Parkinson, founded by John Parkinson in 1894, was already responsible for many of the city's great landmarks, including the Los Angeles Athletic Club (1911), the Memorial Coliseum (1923), and City Hall (with Albert C. Martin doing structural design and John C. Austin the working drawings, 1928) and later Union Station (1939).

John Parkinson was born in 1861 in Scorton, a tiny village in Lancashire County, England. He went to

work at 16, apprenticed to a builder in nearby Bolton where he learned the meaning of craftsmanship and gained a strong knowledge of practical construction. Simultaneously, he attended night school, where he developed architectural drafting and engineering skills. By all accounts he was a master draftsman.

Upon completion of his apprenticeship at age 21, he emigrated to North America as an adventure, where he built fences in Winnipeg and learned stair-building in Minneapolis. Parkinson hoped to continue his career back home, but when he returned to England he found

Donald B. Parkinson

John Parkinson

The original Bullock's store at Seventh Street and Broadway in Los Angeles designed by John Parkinson. Soon after it opened, Bullock's had to weather the financial panic of 1907.

the parochial construction trades unwilling to recognize the skills he had learned overseas.

Parkinson became fed up with the professional rejection he faced in England, and, in a defining moment of his young life, decided to return to America. Parkinson's grandson, Marty Trent of San Pedro, later said that when his grandfather received the final rebuff from the architectural establishment in his homeland, he looked up and saw a painting on the wall of San Francisco Bay, which inspired him to leave at once for the United States to seek his fortune.

Parkinson traveled to California and first settled in Napa. In 1890, he moved to Seattle, where he opened his first architectural practice. He served as School Board Architect from 1891-94, and designed numerous schools there. Today, four buildings remain of his

Seattle accomplishments. Within three years, a serious economic depression hit Seattle. Faced with no projects nor prospects for work, John Parkinson moved on to Los Angeles and opened his architecture office on Spring Street between Second and Third streets.

By 1896, Parkinson had designed the city's first Class "A", fireproof steel-frame structure: the Homer Laughlin Building at Third Street and Broadway. His design for the 1904 Braly Block at Fourth Street and Spring became the first "skyscraper" built in Los Angeles. Rising to a height of more than 173 feet, the novel 12-story building opened to great acclaim and established John Parkinson as the region's leading architect. It held the distinction of being the tallest structure in town until the completion of City Hall 24 years later.

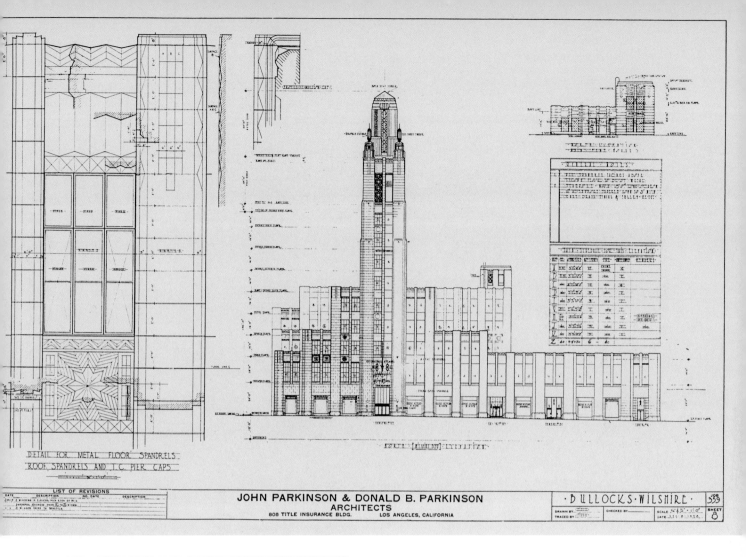

DETAIL FOR METAL FLOOR SPANDRELS
ROOF SPANDRELS AND T.C. PIER CAPS

LIST OF REVISIONS				
DATE	DESCRIPTION	NO.	DATE	DESCRIPTION

JOHN PARKINSON & DONALD B. PARKINSON
ARCHITECTS
808 TITLE INSURANCE BLDG.   LOS ANGELES, CALIFORNIA

· BULLOCKS · WILSHIRE ·

SHEET 8

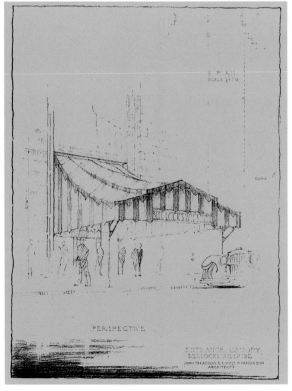

An early Parkinson sketch envisioned a canvas awning instead of a porte cochere for Bullock's Wilshire.

No. 13   TAKEN 5-1-29

BULLOCK'S WILSHIRE BUILDING
JOB No. 384

JOHN PARKINSON &   P. J. WALKER CO
DONALD B. PARKINSON   BUILDERS
ARCHITECTS

Above left:
Excavation for Bullock's Wilshire began in 1928. Located at 3050 Wilshire Boulevard near present-day MacArthur Park, the enterprise was hailed as the first suburban department store and the first to cater to the automobile.

Above right:
Builder P. J. Walker Co. laid the foundation for the department store. 8,000 barrels of cement were used in construction of the five-story steel-reinforced concrete building.

Left:
The steel girder skeleton of Bullock's Wilshire begins to take shape in 1929. John and Donald Parkinson, father and son, served as the building's architects.

Facing page:
Design of the entire structure was affected by the architects' plan to create a landmark 241-foot tower. The advertising value of the tower paid off handsomely and it became the signature stamp of Bullock's Wilshire.

38

In 1905, Parkinson formed a partnership with G. Edwin Bergstrom that lasted for 10 years. Parkinson and Bergstrom became the dominant architectural firm for major structures in Los Angeles. Five years after Bergstrom left to establish his own practice, John Parkinson was joined in 1920 by his son, Donald B. Parkinson.

The relationship between the father and son was highly productive. Together the two men designed dozens of the city's most enduring landmarks, including the original campus of the University of Southern California, begun in 1919, the Los Angeles Memorial Coliseum at Exposition Park in 1923, and the Title Insurance Building located at 433 South Spring Street in downtown Los Angeles in 1929. Built for the leading title and mortgage company in Los Angeles, the latter structure represented one of the finest examples of the Art Deco style to have been built in Los Angeles. Aptly nicknamed the "Queen of Spring Street," the elegant structural composition of refined architectural detailing and glistening terra cotta exterior became a Los Angeles showpiece. The building was such a success that the Parkinson firm was retained five more times over the next 22 years to provide designs for the fast-growing company.

Despite the ability of the Parkinsons to deliver remarkable achievements in architecture to their clients, at times the father and son relationship was taxing. According to his grandson, John Parkinson believed children should be seen and not heard. He was described as emotionally remote from his children. "He wasn't an outgoing, huggy guy," says Marty Trent of his grandfather. "But he was a very loyal, loving person."

The younger Parkinson, Donald, was a masterful artist, formally educated at the Massachusetts Institute of Technology. He married Grace Wells, an accomplished sculptor who shared his love of things artistic. Though he was generally quiet and self-contained, Donald had a passion for fast cars and he had a collection of them parked in different garages. Parkinson even purchased the "Mormon Meteor," a huge race car that had just set the land speed record on the Bonneville

Salt Flats in Utah. Trent recalls Donald Parkinson picking up Trent's pretty young sister — Parkinson's niece — for an evening of carousing in the famous racing car.

John Parkinson was an outdoorsman fond of hard physical exercise. He kept his six-foot-two frame at a lean 140 pounds by working out and walking great distances for pleasure. He also enjoyed singing in his church choir.

John Parkinson was proud that he, without formal education, had a cadre of skilled draftsmen and designers working for him. In the later years of their partnership, John concentrated on bringing in new business while Donald supervised the daily details of the design team.

John Parkinson had visited and studied many classic buildings in Europe, including English cathedrals. He liked to take old concepts and give them a new twist, while Donald had a keenly developed artistic sensibility and had absorbed the latest European designs.

Their extraordinary synergy as architects, though, was highly evident in all of their designs, and the father and son were credited with transforming the city's urban landscape. Bullock and Winnett knew John Parkinson well, having retained him to design the first Bullock's downtown in 1906 as well as subsequent additions. The firm became the obvious choice to design and build the new store.

The original plans for the Wilshire Boulevard store called for elegance within a traditional framework, but a visit by Winnett and the younger Parkinson to an exhibition in Paris in 1925 radically changed the store's initial design.

Winnett's avant-garde taste in fashion caused him to travel to France frequently to view the couture collections. After he had visited the showrooms at Chanel and Schiaparelli and Vionnet, Winnett visited the museums and galleries. Winnett was "inside the delivery room at the Exposition des Arts Decoratifs et Moderne when Art Deco was born," one reporter said. "He liked what he saw and wanted it for his store in Los Angeles."

The exposition that so dazzled Winnett and Donald Parkinson was a trade show the French had been planning before the interruption of World War I. By 1925, the style had evolved into what is now considered Art Deco. The fair showcased interior products such as carpets, furniture, draperies and decorative objects. Housing the products were pavilions that interpreted the style architecturally, and while many of the buildings were seen as impractical, they were exceptional pieces of art that set the stage for a playful new architectural design movement.

And it fit the upbeat mood of the world at the time. The 1920s were prosperous. America was in an expansive mood and undergoing a social revolution. Women now had the right to vote and to smoke. Hemlines were rising and cumbersome undergarments were abandoned. Prohibition made drinking a forbidden thrill, and spirits flourished in speakeasies and private clubs. The rising stock market brought affluence, and easy money and extravagance were commonplace. Art Deco was exuberant, luxurious and elegant, fitting the era and the people's frame of mind. It was the perfect marriage of design and lifestyle, especially in maturing Los Angeles — a fun architectural style for a fun city. Some called Art Deco "Jazz Style." The French called it "Art Moderne."

When Winnett returned from Europe, he scrapped the drawing board plans for Bullock's Wilshire and worked closely with John and Donald Parkinson to create a revolutionary concept of art-in-business that was a radical departure for retailing. The design would incorporate some of the Art Deco expression to be seen in the Parkinsons' Spring Street building constructed for the Title Insurance and Trust Company.

Following Winnett's and Parkinson's return from Paris, the men were filled with enthusiasm for the bold new ideas and designs presented there. The result was a fresh, inspired Art Deco design for Bullock's Wilshire that would simultaneously embrace Los Angeles' new passion, the automobile.

The distinctive tower planned for the building would draw clientele from surrounding residential areas. Large plate glass windows were envisioned to attract passing motorists. The main entrance to the building would be in the rear, adjacent to a landscaped parking lot. In a layout never utilized before, the grand porte cochere, adorned with a fabulous mural, was conceived to provide important customers the "ultimate sense of arrival."

The massive architectural project was completed by a collaboration of the best local designers, sculptors and artists, who converged to create the Art Deco masterpiece. Designer Jock Peters, decorator Eleanor Le Maire, and the design firm of Feil & Paradise created sumptuous, high-style interiors that soon became the talk of the town. The result at Bullock's Wilshire was an artistic modern cathedral, a crowning achievement for the Parkinson firm.

THE DESIGNER

Few, if any, would have been better qualified to produce the themes visualized by Winnett for the interior of Bullock's Wilshire than the man who got the job — Jock Peters. Credit for the artistic designs of many of the store's interiors belongs to the German-born designer, whose modernist style was tempered by his experiences in World War I and a brief stint as a Hollywood art director for Paramount Pictures.

Peters is best known for his extraordinary designs of the signature first two floors of Bullock's Wilshire. His highly lauded work led to commissions to design the interior of Hollander's, a women's specialty store in New York City, more movie sets and a handful of buildings in Southern California, but his premature death in 1934, at the age of 45, thwarted him from achieving the artistic notoriety he so richly deserved.

Peters' success as an architect was no doubt a surprise to his father, who was dismayed when his eldest son showed a keen interest in art. During the early years of Peters' life, the family eked out a hard living on a farm in northern Germany close to the Danish border. Peters was a sensitive boy who feared electrical storms and disliked the pounding ocean. Peters hated the drudgery of farm life and, when he was nine years old, his father failed at farming and moved the family to the

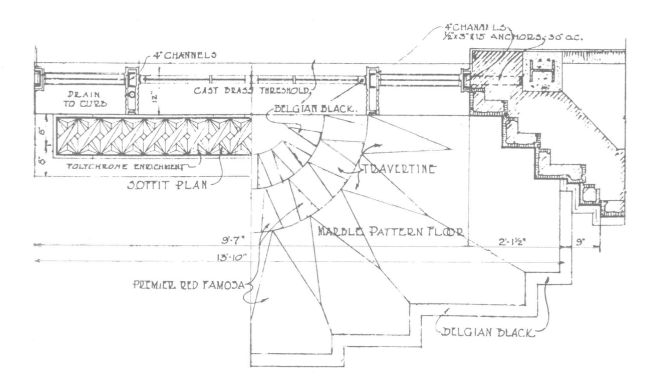

city, where Peters' artistic tendencies began to take root. He spent all his spare time drawing pictures and announced that he intended to become an artist. He soon decided to become an architect, but his father disapproved. A compromise was struck and Peters was apprenticed at age 14 to a stone mason in Hamburg, Germany. Peters thought he might become a sculptor, but his father thought his apprenticeship would lead to something more prosaic—his own tombstone shop adjacent to the local graveyard.

Peters worked in stone for four years under a severe master, finally earning his Journeyman's Letter from the Alliance of German Building Trades Masters in April 1907. Next came more hard study and occasional humiliation at the Baugewerksschule (Building Trades School). Peters once confided to an interviewer that his work there was held up to fellow students as a horrible example. The teacher believed Peters was incapable of understanding the principles of architecture. To his surprise, Peters passed his final exam with a perfectly executed, classic design.

Above:
Polychrome paring and soffit detail of Wilshire Boulevard entrance.

Opposite page:
The porte cochere attended by uniformed valets made Bullock's Wilshire the first department store designed around the automobile.

Jock Peters

This sketch from Jock Peters' project diary shows the concept for decoration on the columns in the Accessories Department at left.

Work as a draftsman for other architects led to what was for Peters an ideal position. In 1913 he went to work for Dr. Peter Behrens, a leading pioneer of the progressive movement in architecture that appealed so much to the young man's artistic sensibilities. Peters spent two years with Behrens, and bolstered his own reputation by winning first prize in a competition to design an electrical power plant in Hamburg.

World War I interrupted this period of promise. Peters was drafted in 1914, but refused active duty as a conscientious objector. He was assigned instead to work

in a munitions repair plant on the Belgian front. In letters to his wife, Herta, whom he married in 1913, Peters revealed the suffering of his creative and intellectual spirit in the harsh military culture. Tragically, he was also exposed to orange gas, and lost one lung to tuberculosis just before the war ended in 1918. Still, he had continued to design during the war, and entered several important competitions. One entry that earned first place was a design for an exhibition tower to honor war heroes to be constructed at the Schiller Memorial in Hamburg. It was never built.

Peters' design career got back on track in 1920, when he was appointed director of the University of Kunstgewerbeschule, the State School for Applied Arts. While he succeeded in restoring the struggling school's reputation, Germany's political and economic disintegration and his own poor health weighed heavily on him. His brother, George, who had emigrated to Southern California before the war and he enticed Peters to follow with the promise of a gentle climate and abundant professional opportunities.

In 1923, Peters sailed for New York, leaving his wife and five children behind. He did not speak English and his architecture credentials were not recognized in America. He was 33.

Peters came directly to Los Angeles and sent for his family after finding a home for them in Eagle Rock. Peters found work as a draftsman with a German architect in Los Angeles, but the pay was poor. A better living was to be found in the movie business, and Peters went to work as an architect and art director with the Famous Players/Lasky Corporation (Paramount Pictures) between 1924 and 1927.

He found studio work hard and felt his true abilities were repressed by Hollywood. In 1927, Peters re-entered the design field, forming a firm with his brother George called Peters Brothers Modern American Design. That year he won first prize in a national competition in furniture design and in 1928 received another first prize in a nationwide rug design contest.

His star was rising. After winning the second prize, Peters explained the term "modernism" for a magazine interviewer: "Art of every kind has a double job to do. First, it must be pleasing in itself. Second, it must present a faithful picture of the times in which it was produced. Good art — the kind of art that lasts for ages — always does just this. It invariably mirrors life as it is being lived ... Through the art that is being produced today, future generations will come to know us."

What Peters wanted future generations to know was that 1920s America was moving at a pace he found breathless. Where previous generations of artists found inspiration in the forms of nature, the modern artist would find his imagery instead in this fast-paced, crowded urban world. Peters, for example, would turn the geometric patterns he saw in a street corner of asphalt and concrete into an abstract motif. The modern, well-balanced design or architectural detail must be restrained and disciplined, said Peters, its crudeness as refined as the "traffic in the heart of the densest city."

"For the underlying principles of art, of design, are changeless; only the inspiration changes," Peters wrote. "And this, fundamentally, is what we mean by 'modernism' — changed inspiration."

THE DECORATOR

Peters came recommended by the highly regarded Eleanor Le Maire, a strong proponent of using the most *au courant* styles. She had been Bullock's decorator since P.G. Winnett hired her in 1926 to make over the downtown store. Le Maire was considered such an extraordinary talent that the Los Angeles Times wrote that she "feels, breathes, [and] lives color and beauty." Le Maire had already made her mark in New York and would return there with Peters in 1931 to design the Hollander store with the Bullock's Wilshire look.

Under the title of coordinator, Le Maire commissioned 13 artists, famous and unknown, to carry out the elegant theme envisioned by P.G. Winnett. George

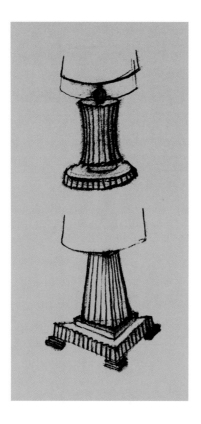
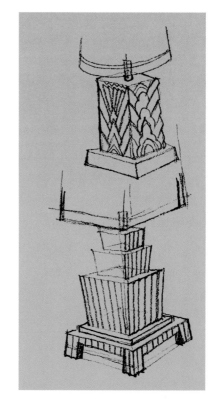

Lamp studies from Peters' project diary.

Stanley, Gjura Stojano, Herman Sachs, Jallot, Eugene Maier Kreig, Laursat, Sonia Delaunay and George De Winter were some of the talented artists selected by Le Maire to create each thematic element as a work of beauty and distinction. Le Maire also utilized the talents of designers David Collins and John Weber in creation of the store's second-floor interiors. In concert with Peters, Le Maire built a special workshop with close to 100 skilled artisans to create the exact effects in metal, wood, glass, tapestries and leather that the team desired.

The critics were so enthralled with the results that Le Maire had achieved that one commentator wrote that Bullock's Wilshire was Le Maire's "best undertaking," and that by working in harmony with the Parkinsons, Peters, De Winter, Weber and Collins she had achieved "a creation of restrained splendor, mental harmony, [and] entrancing beauty. Not a false note anywhere. She has been able to materialize what Mr. Bullock and Mr. Winnett mentally envisioned for this, their mighty project."

THE DESIGN FIRM

Sharing official design credit with Peters was the local design firm of Feil & Paradise, which Bullock and Winnett had hired prior to Peters' arrival. The firm, led by senior partner Joseph L. Feil, was well respected in Los Angeles, having designed such other stores as Silverwood's, Desmond's, and Wetherby Kaysers.

The firm specialized in the design of storefronts and interiors and had earlier transformed the interior of the Collegiene Room at Bullock's downtown store. The resounding artistic success of the central foyer on the ground floor of Bullock's Wilshire was due in large measure to the association of Feil & Paradise with the team of other artists, manufacturers and craftsmen.

THE BUILDERS

The modernist leanings of Peters and Le Maire were reflected in the local and international artists Le Maire hired to put spectacular finishes in the shell built by the contracting firm of P.J. Walker Co.

Architectural woodworking was completed by the Frank Groves Sash, Door & Mill Company, cabinetry by the Commercial Fixture Company, and work in granite was done by the McGilvray Raymond Corporation. Metal showcases were built by the Cochran Company, lathing and plastering was completed by J.F. Bolster & Company, lighting fixtures were supplied by Solar Lighting Fixture Company, Inc., and ornamental iron and bronze hollow metal doors were made by the A.J. Bayer Company. The intricate store fixtures were built by the Vernon Fixture & Cabinet Company and the Weber Showcase & Fixture Company, Inc. The striking entrance to the store clothed in rough-hewn ashlar terra cotta was the creation of the renowned Gladding, McBean & Company, from tiny Lincoln, California, which also had created the artistry seen on the exteriors of the black-clad Richfield Building, City Hall and Los Angeles Theater located in downtown Los Angeles.

THE CRITICS' REACTION

The team responsible for assembling this premier Art Deco building received great accolades for its work, and the striking efforts of the interior designers were widely heralded.

The $2 million store received instant recognition. Pauline G. Schindler, wife of famed Austrian-born architect Rudolph Schindler, wrote in the January 1930 edition of California Arts & Architecture:

"Bullock's Wilshire is a significant contribution to the culture of our generation. It will affect a revolutionary development in taste in southern California, which will eventually penetrate to the more conservative north, and will strongly modify the development of architecture.

"It constitutes an unmistakable advance in the movement of contemporary design. Much of its effect is due to color and light; and it must be actually seen for its artistic significance to be realized.

"Not one or two, but a number of different persons worked together in creating this extended and complicated series of compositions, which constitutes a small village of specialty shops."

San Francisco-based architect Harris Allen wrote, "There is so much that is beauty — even the conservative, however reluctantly, must admit to this point — so little that is bizarre, so much that is refined, so little that is crude, that it constitutes for this region, at least, an architectural landmark."

The modern art editor of The Architect and Engineer magazine, William I. Garren, pronounced in December 1929:

"To my mind it is one of the most consistently modern creations in large retail stores in the country."

John Bullock was so pleased with the efforts of the design team that he ran a beautifully illustrated full-page advertisement in the Los Angeles Times thanking the artists for their contribution to his store and to the cultural heritage of Los Angeles.

"That there may be no misunderstanding, Bullock's Wilshire was designed and planned and constructed nearly in its entirety by Los Angeles talent and of Los Angeles material. Bullock's congratulates Los Angeles upon its possession of artists and artisans of such rare and varied ability as to have been able to principally confine the execution as well as the conception of Bullock's Wilshire within the limits of its own city. For Bullock's Wilshire was designed by Los Angeles architects and made of steel, terra cotta, bronze, brass, sheet metal, glass, wood, cement, concrete, almost everything that has gone into Bullock's Wilshire has come out of the resources of Los Angeles to bend under the will and direction of Los Angeles masters of building, design arrangement and decoration—and to create a new kind of service to serve under the banner of the Bullock Ideal—'Service toward Satisfaction of Every Customer.'

"Bullock's Wilshire—to have been not only visioned and visualized in Los Angeles but built by Los Angeles —as have all of Bullock's Buildings been planned and built and furnished by Los Angeles as far as possible in the years gone by. The resources of Los Angeles are great and are receiving world-wide recognition."

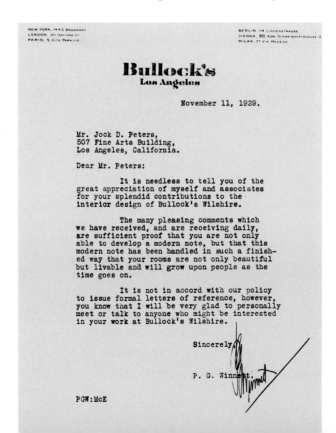

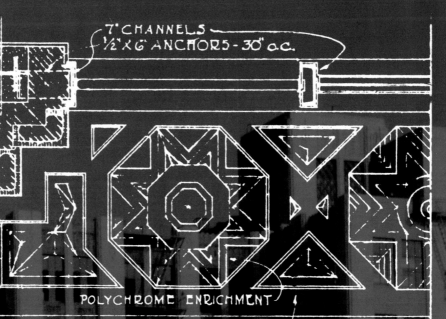

CHAPTER

4

7" CHANNELS
½"X6' ANCHORS-30"o.c.

POLYCHROME ENRICHMENT
REFLECTED CL'G. PLAN

PLAN OF ENTRANCE No.3

INSIDE THE CATHEDRAL

The Los Angeles artisans had produced a patron's dream. Whether entered from the broad sweep of the motor court or from the impressive terra cotta faced facade of the Wilshire Boulevard entrance, the visual effect was the same — a series of magnificent vistas, viewed through graceful arches in polished marble and striped with golden mirrors.

A customer's first steps inside the store placed him in the high-domed foyer, where the Bauhaus-themed design of the elevator doors was framed in bronze, copper and gunmetal. The elevator floor indicators were designed to look like years passing, bringing forward the notion of movement introduced in the porte cochere. Even the clock nearby on the south wall exhibited the bold industrial flair and Bauhaus love of machinery, complete with gear-like sprockets in the clock's minute hand.

Ahead was the dramatic perfume hall, likened by California Arts & Architecture critic Harris Allen to a great marble basilica. "That sounds cold, formal, austere," he wrote. "Nothing could be further from the truth. These lofty walls (which are of a western stone called St. Genevieve Rose Marble) are glowing with warmth and color — more like onyx than marble. The air is full of light, but there is no glare. None of the ordinary evidences of commerce are visible; the low

Left:
The stunning fresco-seco ceiling of
the porte cochere mural by artist
Herman Sachs was called "Spirit
of Transportation" and depicted
transport in the '20s and '30s. It
was lovingly restored by famed
muralist Heinsbergen in 1973.

Below:
One of the thirty imaginative
clocks created for the store.

Above:
The Bauhaus style elevator doors inside the store's
grand foyer used bronze, copper and gunmetal.

Right:
The Perfume Hall, which one critic called "a great
marble basilica." The mirrors and lights created
entrancing effects throughout the store.

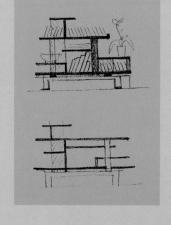

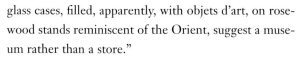

glass cases, filled, apparently, with objets d'art, on rose-wood stands reminiscent of the Orient, suggest a museum rather than a store."

Designer Jock Peters accented the Perfume Hall's light panels with vertical, metallic strips, creating a soft glow and welcoming ambiance.

East of the elevator foyer lay an alcove for purses, shoes and accessories. The original chandeliers were tube-shaped, illuminating a room accented in pastels of pale tan, pink and robin's egg blue. The room was broken into intimate departments and accented with rugs by French Cubist artist Sonya Dealunay.

West of the main hall was the Sportswear department, where the designers successfully captured a sense of speed, movement and modernity. Key to the drama was a mural on the west wall entitled "Spirit of Sports," a glittering, angular abstract interpretation flavored by

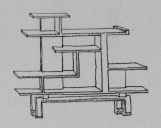

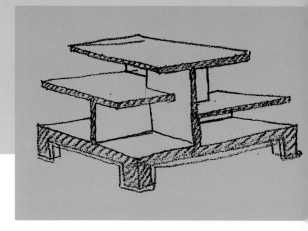

Facing page:
The Sportswear Department was designed to reflect a sense of
casual freedom of the out-of-doors for upscale buyers.
Its thematic mural called "The Spirit of Sports" was one of the
most beautiful pieces of art in the store. Created by artist Gjura
Stojano it was an expression of action, speed and movement
and consisted of a flat fresco with plaster relief and thin strips
of wood veneer.

Gifts Department with study
sketches for display cases from
Peters' project diary.

the German Bauhaus style. The Los Angeles Times reported in 1929 that the artist, Gjura Stojano, placed a small cot inside the room so that he could "live his work."

Also on the first floor was the Saddle Shop. Here, Jock Peters interpreted the International Style popular at the time in France and Germany with interlocking cubic volumes. Vertical panels on the west wall were an abstract reference to stables. The floor was covered in a brick-like vermilion tile and a hand-woven rug with colors of deep browns and orange-red. Wall cases of dark,

red oak stood under a playful plaster relief by Eugene Maier-Krieg depicting polo players, archers and animals.

Horse owner and enthusiast Winnett enjoyed one special feature of the original Saddle Shop. In the corner was a stall for a life-sized plaster horse known as "Bullock's Barney," where patrons could climb up and check the fit of their jodhpurs.

Strategically placed atop a switch-back stairway above the Saddle Shop was the playful Doggery, where the latest finery from collars to sweaters could be found for man's best friend. Perhaps nowhere was the combined whimsy of both the designers and merchants more evident.

Also on the mezzanine was the Playdeck, originally the site for swimwear and "play" clothes. Winnett and Bullock's were pioneers in the growth of California's sportswear industry by introducing poolside wear, beach pajamas, sunsuits and other leisure-oriented women's wear.

When the building opened, there was a patio and children's play area outside the southwest corner of the building where the little ones could play while parents shopped. The Courtyard disappeared in the 1940's

Above:
Plaster reliefs by artist Maier-Krieg enlivened the walls of the Saddle Shop and depicted hurdlers, polo players and a child riding a comet's tail. The room was conceived in colors of dark fumed oak and russet with a ceiling checkered in blue and gray, buff and maroon. Brick patterned rugs adorned the floors.

Right:
Stairs led from the Saddle Shop to the Doggery, a whimsical pet department where the latest modes in dog collars, sweaters and accessories were sold.

when it was incorporated into the building as an addition to the Menswear department.

Until then, the Palm Court was an open room leading to the Courtyard. After the renovation, a new Palm Court with palm trees made of gold metal was created in what was originally a lounge and smoking area.

The Menswear Department was a series of suites with a distinctly masculine tone. Peters successfully adapted architect Frank Lloyd Wright's concrete block style, an important influence at the time, which evoked Mayan temples. There was an emphasis on rectilinear forms, with rough, tan plastered walls juxtaposed with patterned borders. Even the light pattern was geometric. Spatially there was an effective division of vertical and horizontal areas that increased privacy while creating a sense of openness.

The architectural style in Menswear was a tribute to Frank Lloyd Wright. Treatment of the wall surfaces and the manipulation of space were dramatic adaptations of Wright's renowned concrete block houses.

Eleanore Le Maire's stylish touch was evident on the second floor, home to the "Period Rooms," high-fashion salons evoking 18th and 19th century France. Fine designer dresses were sold in the Louis XVI Room, a free interpretation of Marie Antoinette's boudoir in ivory walls, gold molding and crystal chandeliers.

The Directoire was intended to resemble a private drawing room of the period and originally sold formal and evening wear, later becoming the Fur Salon. It was an extremely intimate room where details included a fireplace, murals of Paris monuments by George De Winter, classicized molding, and garlands. The murals simulated early 19th century block-printed wallpaper in the directoire style. Doors with a bow-and-arrow design led to the dressing rooms. To simulate conditions under which finery purchased there would be worn, lights would be dimmed as models appeared in the gowns.

There was also a Louis XV room that sold fine accessories. It was styled in French rococo with George De Winter wall paintings intended to look like wood panels. It later became the Chanel Room, featuring couture by Coco Chanel and guarded by Chanel's trade-mark bronze monkeys in the doorway. Also inside the French Room, as the space became known, was a lounge fashioned after Josephine's bathroom at Malmaison.

Warm tones of ivory and gold, sparkling chandeliers and gilded accents created the regal Louis XVI Period Room where fine designer dresses were viewed. The setting was intended as an interpretation of Marie Antoinette's boudoir at the Petit Trianon at Versailles, France.

The collaboration of Peters and Feil & Paradise resulted in one of the store's unique rooms, the elegant and sophisticated Fur Atelier, with cork board walls, dull pink ceiling and oyster-gray center panel. The floor was designed in checkered random blocks and seats were covered in brilliant coral velours edged with Chinese vermilion. Opal glass lanterns with silver rings and black tassels hung from the ceiling.

Also on the second floor was Ladies Lingerie, a delightfully feminine interpretation of the Art Deco style. Recessed lights and moldings created geometric patterns reflecting pink from a wall of special glass called Vitralite. Considered an obsolete material now,

Above right:
Patrons selecting furs in the sophisticated setting of the Fur Atelier were seated on lavishly upholstered sofas made of brilliant coral velour edged in Chinese vermilion.

Right:
The Fur Atelier was considered one of the store's most extraordinary rooms. The walls were covered in cork in sumptuous shades of brown. Opal-glass lanterns with tassels hung from the ceiling.

The Boudoir, before the creation of Irene's Salon.

Vitralite was introduced in the early 20th century as a glass, usually white or black, that was meant to look like carrara marble.

The dramatic "Studio of Beauty," which was never considered a mere "beauty salon," was located on the second floor as well. Among its original features were synthetic marble plumbing features, 18 stations for stylists and a permanent wave setting machine that looked like something out of a science fiction fantasy. A special room offered suntans from ultra-violet lights in an early version of a tanning booth.

Reports through the years differ on whether Jock Peters had a hand in design of the third floor, or whether it was the work of another store designer named David Collins, but it is clearly a departure from the individualized treatment of the boutique departments on the first two floors. When the building

A proper permanent wave required a formidable machine.

An early tanning bed in the Salon of Beauty.

Facing page:
The Tea Room with its fashion shows was one of Bullock's Wilshire's greatest traditions and drew successive generations of Los Angeles women, who took their daughters as their mothers had taken them.

Left:
Beautifully displayed toys delighted children in the toy department.

Below left:
Children's play area outside the southwest corner of the roof.

Below:
Cribs for the well-born.

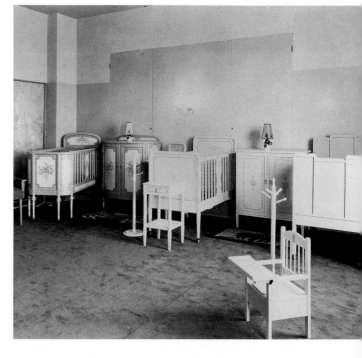

opened, the third floor served college and high school girls. Architectural Record magazine described a setting of natural color walnut, maple and satin wood, with carpet patterns and ceiling panels designed to aid the movement of foot traffic from room to room.

Collins is recognized as the fourth-floor designer. This was the children's floor, with many small rooms — such as the book and toy departments, and children's and infants' wear. No juvenile need went unattended: there was a Mothers' and Children's Restroom, a Mothers' Retiring Room for diaper changes and nursing, a Maids' Room and even a barber shop.

John Weber had the vision for the fifth-floor public spaces. In 1929 the rooms were unified with a California-flavor: the Cactus Room, the Salle Moderne and the Tea Room. Quite Deco, the rooms joined thematically with the first two floors. The ceiling was a series of squares used as structure, ornament and lighting, fusing rational structure with decoration. The largest dining room was the Salle Moderne, a Bauhaus

64

design with a color scheme that might be considered Southwestern today: gray with accents in pink, blue green and tan. Desert animals painted on lacquered panels by Maurice Jallot adorned the walls and an abstract cactus design in grillwork highlighted the windows. A grille of copper, forming a stylized cactus plant, separated the elevator lobby from the Cactus Room. The glass ceiling filtered light through a pattern of soft green hues that echoed the cactus theme. The floors were colored in taupe and sand, and the walls were painted sage and olive.

Also on the fifth floor was a confectionery and what was originally John Bullock's office, with beautiful oak-paneled walls, a plaster ceiling cast in Tudor style and a balcony terrace. The space saw a variety of uses through the years, including the display of fine porcelain and an employee lounge.

The Tea Room opened from one side of the lobby with a series of connecting rooms for luncheons, banquets and teas, each unique in its decorative scheme in tones of green, gold and tan. Panels depicting California deer adorned the walls of the assembly room. Inside, custom made chairs and couches were upholstered in exquisite fabrics that created an atmosphere of tranquility.

The store's Tower, the outstanding crescendo to the building's architecture, was once crowned by a mercury beacon that formed a striking silhouette against the California sunset. The spectacular 241-foot spire with its majestic blue-green light was intended to lure customers to the store, but it became Bullock's Wilshire's most singular trademark. Illuminated by 88 floodlights and four neon mercury vapor tubes and powered by 39,000 watts of electricity, the copper-crested tower with its blue-hued light could be seen in Los Angeles' skyline from miles away.

Conceived as both a landmark and an advertising display, architects John and Donald Parkinson cleverly pushed building laws to the limit to achieve the tower's mass and height. City ordinances restricted building

View from fifth floor Salle Moderne through the Cactus Room with the elevator foyer beyond

This lamp study seen next to the building's overall massing shows how architecture and interiors were seamlessly integrated and mutually inspired.

heights to 150 feet, but allowed in addition six feet of roof construction, 35 feet of penthouse construction and 50 feet of sign construction, making a total legal height of 241 feet. The penthouse structure could only be used for water tanks and machinery, while the sign was to be used strictly for advertising. Sign materials were limited to sheet metal and light steel members, a restriction which, to a great extent, determined the design of the entire building.

The architects decided against painting the upper 50 feet of the tower in imitation of the terra cotta masonry used in the lower stories of the building. Instead, the metal finish of the sign structure was carried throughout the lower exterior in the ornamentation of the spandrels, which dictated to a great extent the actual forms the Parkinsons used in their design, as well as the colors. The green of oxidized copper from the sign structure combined nicely with buff-colored terra cotta panels cladding the steel-framed structure.

The Tower was designed and engineered to allow future vertical expansion of the store by as many as five more floors around the tower. The Parkinsons endeavored to make the exterior design reflect its skeleton and to confine ornamentation to geometric patterns.

Left:
The Millinery Department was decorated in warm tones of pinkish-cream, jade green and pumpkin. A soft thick patterned carpet in dark blue-green hues covered the floor.
The light fixtures inside the Millinery Department were shimmering, delicate showers of clear and frosted glass trimmed in silvered metal.

Below:
The Etchings Department.

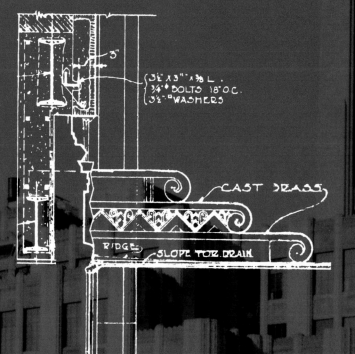

(3½"×3"×½L.
¾"♦ BOLTS 18"O.C.
(3½"□ WASHERS

3"

CAST BRASS

RIDGE

SLOPE TO DRAIN

IN HOLLYWOOD'S EMBRACE

Bullock's Wilshire was our only emporium. Beverly Hills had no department stores then, Rodeo Drive was just a lazy street in a pretty palm-treed village that Laurel and Hardy used as a backdrop. So, one ventured forth by chauffeured car to Hollywood on Wilshire Boulevard, not quite as far as downtown Los Angeles, but nearly, and there it was — our version of the Chrysler Building! Not as tall, not as majestic; you couldn't really visualize King Kong clinging to its sides, but in a town of one-storied haciendas, clapboard bungalows, and fruit-juice stands in the shape of oranges, it was your ten-story skyscraper, all Art Deco, carved concrete, and triangular glass. The doorman, resplendent in the Bullock's colors of bitter chocolate and beige, ushered us through the ornate glass doors. Harry and the green Rolls remained parked directly in front of the store; then, the streets were always empty. The vaulted main floor looked like a French cathedral —they could have used it for The Hunchback of Notre Dome. It was awesome.

— MARIA RIVA,
DAUGHTER OF MARLENE DIETRICH

John Bullock's daring experiment in merchandising and the bold temple he built to house it became a glorious adventure that proved enormously profitable. Never before had the citizens of Los Angeles been invited to trade under such sumptuous conditions. Every last detail for a customer's complete satisfaction had been considered and delivered. The great store's dedication to style, decor and service ensured its place at the top of the roster for the city's fashionable elite, and soon the store became the shopping destination for Hollywood's biggest stars.

The world's best fashion designers were featured on the second floor at Bullock's Wilshire, where each exquisite department was complete in itself. Evening gowns created by such famous names as Chanel, Cristobal, Blass, Courreges, de la Renta, Dior, Galanos, Givenchy, Halston, Saint-Laurent, and Schiaparelli were shown by live models, known as "mannequins," in the Louis XVI Period Room or in the adjoining Directoire as patrons remained seated and made their selections. The rooms were often darkened during fashion shows so that customers could see the fine gowns in "simulated evening light." The neoclassical design of the fine apparel rooms with their warm ivory and gold tones, sparkling chandeliers and gilded accents was intended to resemble an early 19th century salon.

Enormous murals evoked a sense of intimacy, serenity and prosperity. Nearby, the elegant Chanel Room featured nothing but the most expensive haute couture creations of designer Coco Chanel. Clothes racks were forbidden, and everything was handsomely displayed on the female form.

A significant remodeling of the Boudoir Accessories department took place on the second floor in 1935 to create the Hollywood-flavored "Irene Salon," where gowns by designer Irene Gibbons were sold. At the time, a simple Irene frock could be purchased for $450. Known simply as "Irene," the highly regarded MGM costume designer created fashions for over 50 films as well as supervising the personal wardrobes of many top stars. She became famous for her "soufflé creations," and is best remembered as the designer who created Lana Turner's provocative white hot pants in the "The Postman Always Rings Twice" (1946).

Irene's Salon became an important fixture at Bullock's Wilshire and was the first boutique inside a large department store devoted to the work of one American designer. Irene's creations were worn on and off the screen by such luminaries as Marlene Dietrich, Rosalind Russell, Claudette Colbert, Loretta Young, Carole Lombard, Ingrid Bergman, Joan Crawford, Paulette Goddard, June Allyson and Ginger Rogers. Irene also created a number of special designs for actress Doris Day, and the pair were often seen shopping together at Bullock's Wilshire, where Day particularly favored the Playdeck.

The dressmaker's original designs became so popular that Irene opened a dress shop at the University of Southern California campus and another a year later in Hollywood. Irene remained on staff at Bullock's Wilshire for seven years. Her salon was closed in 1942 as World War II got under way. After a highly successful career that included lucrative contracts with other leading department stores and two Academy Award nominations for costume design, one in 1948 for "B.F.'s Daughter," and one in 1960 for "Midnight Lace," Irene said that she withdrew from costume design because of an "era of realism" that had been introduced into Hollywood fashion.

Sadly, Irene committed suicide on November 16, 1962, when she jumped to her death from the 11th floor of the Hollywood Knickerbocker Hotel. The 60-year-old designer left several suicide notes that indicated she was distressed over the illness of her husband, screenwriter Eliot Gibbons, who had recently suffered a stroke, and was worried about financial troubles.

Above:
An elaborate display in the elegant Perfume Hall, where customers selected cosmetics from satin finished rosewood display cases.

Right:
George Stanley, the designer most renowned for the Oscar award statuette, created this striking panel over the Wilshire Boulevard entrance.

Left:
An Art Deco drinking fountain outside the Salon of Beauty.

Below:
There were a total of 18 stations for stylists in the Salon of Beauty. Exotic-looking hair dryers await fashionable patrons.

Sales clerks at Bullock's Wilshire recall such luminaries as Clark Gable, Carole Lombard, Greta Garbo, Gloria Swanson, Robert Stack, Katharine Hepburn, Judy Garland, Paulette Goddard, Alfred Hitchcock, Jean Harlow, Agnes Moorehead, David Niven, Ingrid Bergman, Jack Palance, Joan Blondell, Dinah Shore and many others who visited the store to shop. One of the store's favorite celebrity patrons was silent film star ZaSu Pitts, who made grand entrances into Bullock's Wilshire's motor court in her classic Stanley Steamer well into the 1950s.

Anna Frazzini, who began working at Bullock's Wilshire in 1932, remembers a time when Greta Garbo came in wearing a trenchcoat and asked Frazzini to help her select a swimsuit. When the pair entered the fitting room, the actress removed her coat.

"It turns out that's all she was wearing," says Frazzini, who was stunned. "I don't remember whether she bought the suit or not."

Bullock's Wilshire's model Ivana Kislinger Mooney remembers hearing a familiar drawl in the elevator demanding loudly, "Where the hell is the Tea Room and all of those models?" It was the forthright he-man John Wayne on his way to lunch.

Former Bullock's Wilshire president Walter Bergquist, while he was an assistant buyer at the store, saw one image that will last a lifetime. One day he was

Opposite page:
Hollywood's horse and polo crowd selected their riding gear in the Saddle Shop. The Saddle Shop evoked the mood of a fine racing stable and had its own door to Wilshire Boulevard.

Left:
Comic actress ZaSu Pitts enjoyed making a scene by arriving under the porte cochere in her classic Stanley Steamer automobile.

Above, top:
Greta Garbo bought men's suits at Bullock's Wilshire to help create her outrageous fashion statement.

Above, bottom:
John Wayne, one of Hollywood's greatest stars, was a regular guest at Bullock's Wilshire's fifth-floor Tea Room.

instructed to take a pile of coats and suits to Fitting Room 12. Bergquist did as he was told, but when he opened the fitting room door he discovered over-the-rainbow chanteuse Judy Garland sitting on the floor. Naked. Sipping a martini.

Mae West was far more modest. The story has often been repeated that West, who lived in a lavish apartment near Bullock's Wilshire, preferred to do her shopping from the privacy of her car. Salesclerks would carry the merchandise outside of the store to her automobile parked near the motor court, where she would make her selections without the inconvenience of entering the store.

Above, left:
Judy Garland gave a
young assistant buyer the
surprise of his life in a
second-floor fitting room.

Above, right:
Mae West lived near
Bullock's Wilshire and was
a frequent shopper, but
preferred curbside service.

Far left:
Clark Gable and Greta
Garbo were among the
Hollywood stars who
patronized Bullock's
Wilshire.

Left:
Always superbly dressed,
Marlene Dietrich made
Bullock's Wilshire her only
emporium.

The Golden Age of Hollywood coincided neatly with the glory years of Bullock's Wilshire.

A page of Hollywood history from one of the store's elegant press releases:

Q *What mysterious actress in the 1930s was seen trying on trousers in the men's department at Bullock's Wilshire?*

A *Greta Garbo. She bought three pairs.*

Q *Which handsome leading man ordered a paisley wool ski suit from our exclusive fabric selection during WWII, and then had an identical one made for his female companion?*

A *Clark Gable (and Carole Lombard)*

Q *Which famous artist in the 1920s created the "Oscar" award and also sculpted the relief over the Wilshire Boulevard entrance of BW's flagship store?*

A *George Stanley*

Q *Which Hollywood glamour queen in the 1930s kept BW open late while she did her shopping in the Irene Salon?*

A *Marlene Dietrich*

Q *Which famous publisher bought dozens of swimsuits from our Playdeck department to attire his San Simeon house guests?*

A *William Randolph Hearst*

Q *Which sexy film star was a frequent BW shopper yet never set foot into our store? (She had merchandise brought out to her black limousine, which she parked outside the store on Wilshire Boulevard.)*

A *Mae West*

In time, a symbiotic relationship developed between Bullock's Wilshire and Hollywood, so much so that for over 60 years, the store remained a symbol of Hollywood beauty and glamour. Bullock's Wilshire was the city's premier mercantile venue, operated and staffed by colorful personalities, some of whom became famous themselves. Former First Lady Pat Nixon and actresses Angela Lansbury and June Lockhart worked at the store as young sales clerks, among others.

Angela Lansbury came to Bullock's Wilshire in December 1942. She was 16 years old, and lived with her mother in a one-room apartment on Ocean Avenue, where she slept in the kitchen. Hired by P.G. Winnett as a wrapper and cashier for the Christmas season, Lansbury was taught how to painstakingly wrap the "perfect Bullock's box," with unique pleats at the end and special monogram stamp. Asked to stay on as a sales clerk in cosmetics following the seasonal rush, the lovely young English girl with the ivory complexion sold the finest and most expensive cosmetics to some of Los Angeles' most fashionable women, while she used the least expensive drug store brands at home.

Lansbury remembers the feeling of intense pride she experienced as a "young woman working in such a

Above:
Actress Angela Lansbury worked behind the cosmetics counter as a struggling actress before she landed the role as the flirtatious maid Nancy in director George Cukor's 1944 thriller "Gaslight."

Right:
Actress Marion Davies and publisher William Randolph Hearst were seen often at Bullock's Wilshire where they purchased dozens of swimsuits for guests at their famous San Simeon castle-by-the-sea.

beautiful place" and recalls seeing some of Hollywood's biggest stars shopping at Bullock's Wilshire, including Irene Dunne and Barbara Stanwyck. After Lansbury was moved to the handbags department, she watched as publisher William Randolph Hearst entered the store with Marion Davies, who dragged a full-length mink coat behind her on Bullock's Wilshire's marble floor.

Lansbury stayed on until June 1943 when she was asked to make a screen test at MGM Studios. She was signed to a long-term contract and within weeks had landed her first feature role in "Gaslight" (1944), which earned her a first Oscar nomination for Best Supporting Actress. Lansbury would later return to Bullock's Wilshire as a customer and remembers the wonderful welcome she received from her fellow former staffers. Embracing the Bullock's mystique, Lansbury purchased a stunning lavender tweed suit in Bullock's Wilshire's

Sportswear Department in 1945, which she wore as a bride for her first marriage, to actor Richard Cromwell.

(Lansbury's mother, Moyna Macgill, also worked at Bullock's Wilshire on the fourth floor in the toy department, but was eventually let go because she spent too much time lovingly playing with the children and the toys for sale.)

Lansbury subsequently received two more Oscar nominations for "The Picture of Dorian Gray" (1945) and "The Manchurian Candidate" (1962). In 1984, Miss Lansbury began a new phase in her successful career when she undertook the role of Jessica Fletcher, patterned after Agatha Christie's Miss Marple, in the hit TV mystery series, "Murder She Wrote." The program remains one of the most popular American television shows ever and is watched around the world. Lansbury's love for Bullock's Wilshire prompted her to return twice

to shoot episodes of "Murder She Wrote." Presented with original sterling silver sugar and cream dishes from the store's grand Tea Room by Bullock's Wilshire personnel, Lansbury treasures the items as fond keepsakes.

Not only did the stars work at Bullock's Wilshire; the building itself became a star player as well. Bullock's Wilshire's first appearance on the silver screen as a featured setting was in the 1937 comedy "Topper," starring Cary Grant and Constance Bennett. Director Alfred Hitchcock was not only a regular shopper, but he loved the store enough to stage a portion of his last movie, "Family Plot," inside the grand foyer. The Bullock's Wilshire name was obscured but the cosmetic section and Lingerie department figured prominently, and some of Bullock's Wilshire's models appeared behind the counter in the film.

Bullock's Wilshire enjoyed a lucrative career as a prime stage for movies and television. It served as a back drop in the film "Bugsy," starring Warren Beatty and Annette Bening, as well as "Rough Magic," with Bridget Fonda. "The Tie That Binds," starring Daryl Hannah and "The Pack," featuring Mario Van Peebles also utilized the store. Segments of "On Deadly Ground," an action adventure starring Steven Seagal, and an HBO movie starring Alan Alda called "White Mile" used the location. Bullock's famed motor court became the setting for a scene in "White Man's Burden," a 1995 fantasy about the reversal of race relations starring John Travolta and Harry Belafonte. Bullock's Wilshire was also featured prominently in the Faye Dunaway film, "Dunston Checks In." The store has repeatedly served as a backdrop for various music videos and commercials.

The singular relationship between Bullock's Wilshire and Hollywood was perhaps best immortalized during the centennial celebration of Hollywood's first 100 years in 1987, when a giant inflatable King Kong was affixed to the 10-story tower of Bullock's Wilshire attracting hordes of tourists, Hollywood fans and members of the press.

Director Alfred Hitchcock used the store as a location for his 54th and final film, "Family Plot." Written by Ernest Lehman, the 1976 thriller and comedy featured a phony psychic who gets involved in a sinister murder plot hatched by actor William DeVane.

Facing page:
Inside the Salon of Beauty.

CHAPTER

6

THE BULLOCK IDEAL

"To build a business that will never know completion but that will advance continually to meet advancing conditions.

To develop stocks and service to a notable degree.

To create a personality that will be known for its strength and friendliness.

To arrange and co-ordinate activities to the end of winning confidence by meriting it.

To strive always to secure the satisfaction of every customer."

— THE BULLOCK IDEAL

The unique retail philosophy behind Bullock's, conceived by Arthur Letts and refined by John Bullock, was eloquently expressed by the store's advertising director William A. Holt in 1912 when he wrote "The Bullock Ideal." The creed was reprinted thousands of times in employee manuals, annual reports and advertisements and the opening words were handsomely carved above the Wilshire street entrance to the store.

The lengths to which Bullock's staffers would go to satisfy a customer's needs were legendary. It was not uncommon for a messenger to be dispatched with an evening dress needed by nightfall, or a wedding gift, if needed, to be delivered by a store executive. Courtesy and service were mandatory in all of Bullock's stores. Not only was the staff expected to be friendly and solicitous, they were also expected to take whatever steps were required — walk miles if necessary — to see that patrons were satisfied.

As a result of this unusual dedication and resourcefulness, a unique vocabulary was developed and utilized by all employees. It was no ordinary store. As one writer described it, "There were no customers, only patrons. A clerk was a salesperson and an elevator or telephone operator was an elevator or telephone attendant." Classes were conducted for employees in proper

etiquette and service and courtesy were raised to a mandatory art form. Patrons "were to be treated with the [same] courtesy one would show a guest in one's own home."

Author Tom Mohoney, who included John Bullock in his book "The Great Merchants," wrote that the ideals espoused by Bullock's were backed by actions and there was little Bullock's would not do for a customer. John Bullock was said to have once been at the door of his store bidding customers good-bye the evening before St. Patrick's Day when a customer expressed her regret that she had found no clay pipes for an Irish party planned for the next day in Santa Monica. According to Mohoney, Bullock noted her address, had the city scoured for clay pipes and then delivered the items to the amazed customer at her home.

Bullock's personnel also were expected to look the part. For many years, that included a hat and gloves for females entering and leaving the store, and a strict prohibition against the use of nail polish. The staff members were instructed to wear special colors to match different departments. Sales clerks in Sportswear wore brown, inside the Children's Department employees wore beige and in the French Room it was always necessary to wear black.

Bullock's already had a winning reputation when the Wilshire Boulevard store opened in 1929, but Bullock and Winnett went to extraordinary lengths to set Bullock's Wilshire above and apart from the original downtown store, to create a mystique the store would carry to its closing day. The sensational shell and unrivaled decor were only the physical foundation upon which the men built their unique enterprise.

Bullock's Wilshire was a very special place to those who worked there as well as to those who shopped there. One long-term sales clerk said there was "no end to the pride and devotion the employees had for their store and their employer." Once hired at Bullock's Wilshire, employees usually were reluctant to depart,

even to another branch in the chain. Standards were extremely high and employees were expected to live up to them.

When Bullock's Wilshire opened, it was staffed largely by recruits from the Seventh Street store. They, along with the new hires, were selected, Bullock said, on the basis of their culture, poise and fashion appreciation. He and Winnett maintained a staff of almost 700, a number critics pronounced "too high to justify."

"We think it pays," said Bullock. "Our salespeople have time to serve every customer with individual consideration."

Punishment was swift for those employees who didn't measure up to the "Bullock Ideal." If the clerk escaped outright firing, banishment to a less prestigious department or to another store was a likely punishment.

Kiyo Hirayama, an administrative assistant to three Bullock's Wilshire presidents, puts it succinctly: "That was a very special time in our lives. It was not just a job — people felt very personally involved."

A key part of the formula that made Bullock's Wilshire stand out during its glory days was a concept Winnett called "unitization." That meant each store had its own staff of buyers — a luxury few, if any, department stores can afford today. Bullock's Wilshire had as many as 60 of its own buyers and its own merchandise managers, who helped give the store its own personality.

Buyers were expected to know exactly what suited the personal tastes of their patrons and to provide them with a selection they couldn't find anywhere else. Buyers traveled to New York for the debut of each fashion season and stayed up to two weeks looking for just the right lines of merchandise. They sought goods from around the world to bring that certain edge and taste of glamour for which the store was known. Each was also required to spend at least two hours a day on the floor actually selling merchandise with their own sales book.

Buyers also were required to manage their departments as if they were their own stores. They received a

---

Facing page:
A store that wed art to commerce, Bullock's Wilshire gleamed like a jewel along Wilshire Boulevard.

monthly operating sheet that tallied their expenses from maintenance to mark-downs. Winnett wanted his buyers to be "merchants," a term of honor.

The challenge was compounded for Bullock's Wilshire because of its need to bring customers in from great distances. Patrons had to be continuously convinced that they were seeing merchandise they couldn't purchase anywhere else. The store accomplished this with great success through a carefully planned image based on advertising and distinctive graphics.

Bullock's Wilshire dared to be different in its marketing. The exclusive territorial rights to a special modern type face — called "Stellar Bold" — were purchased by the store, and all graphics generated in advertisements, wrapping paper, shopping bags and more were set in this distinctive font. Both Winnett and Bullock made sure that every piece of printing sent out by the store repeated the general theme of the store's stately tower and the handsome lines of the building were suggested in every piece of copy. If color was used, the advertising used the store's prevailing color combinations.

A special artist was trained to produce the drawings that went into Bullock's Wilshire's advertisements, which developed into a characteristic and unmistakable design. The graphics for the store were so successful and considered so attractive, that Bullock's Wilshire advertising was exhibited in 1929 at the Metropolitan Museum of Art in New York City as representative of the "best in modernistic graphics." When asked about the unusual treatment of his carefully crafted advertisements, Bullock said: "Bullock's Wilshire places a high valuation on some of the other intangible elements in business, as well as on art."

Bullock also stressed the importance of other factors he found vital in the creation of the Bullock's Wilshire mystique. These included the value of time, where hundreds of personnel catered to each customer, the value of privacy, where spaces were created for a customer to concentrate undisturbed upon the selection of merchandise, and the value of quiet, whereby the floor plan

and sound-deafening effects of the store ensured freedom from the confusion and noise associated with lesser quality retail stores.

Bullock and Winnett were not afraid to award those who worked diligently to enhance the Bullock's name. One such legendary member who infused buyers and other employees with the Bullock's philosophy was Ann Hodge, one of Winnett's original transferees from the downtown store to Bullock's Wilshire.

Friends who remember Miss Hodge say she loved only three things: the Catholic church, Scotch whisky and Bullock's Wilshire. As general merchandise manager and later the store's first female president, she made it her business to monitor every detail of the store's operation, from window dressings to her employees' clothes. No one was hired in any department who didn't get the nod from Miss Hodge, and "Miss Hodge" is what everyone called her.

"Don't call me Ann. Even my mother calls me Miss Hodge," she reportedly said. The story is probably apocryphal, but her commitment to formality and manners was renowned.

"Ann Hodge was very much the lady," remembers former display designer Kenny Farrow. "Very polite, very firm, and she knew exactly what she wanted. She kept a good rein on everything."

One of the things she wanted was the right kind of person working at Bullock's Wilshire, and that extended to their families as well. Former general manager Richard Rifenbark remembers Miss Hodge standing by the cosmetic case near the west entrance at closing time and taking the measure of her staff as they left. If a woman who recently married was being picked up by her husband, Miss Hodge would walk out to the car and have a look at the new spouse, shooting her bifocals up and down as she made a full appraisal of his suitability as a mate of a Bullock's Wilshire employee.

Another legend has Miss Hodge, as store general manager, becoming piqued with a route boy who made the mistake of coming to work with a fashionable new crewcut hairstyle. She sent him to work in the base-

nent, where patrons wouldn't see him until his hair grew longer.

The force of Miss Hodge's will helped create the Bullock's Wilshire aura, even if it meant overriding buyers' decisions. Her own taste in clothes was limited to basic black, and the gowns made for her by celebrity designer Irene Gibbons always showed off Miss Hodge's shapely legs. Her one bit of vanity was revealed

Critics said that Bullock's Wilshire had achieved the architectural significance of New York City's Chrysler Building. The landmark has been termed "the American version of Parisian Moderne," by authors David Gebhard and Robert Winter.

in her dress orders. She always requested a size 12 and was always shipped a size 16. They always fit.

When Miss Hodge died, she reportedly left more than $1 million to her beloved parish church in the Wilshire District. "She was one of the smartest business women I've ever known, and one of the nicest," says Peggy Smith, a model who went on to manage the millinery department.

Another important personality at Bullock's Wilshire was Agnes Farrell, the store's fashion director and advertising manager from the 1930s well into the 1960s. A petite lady who always was dressed to perfection, Farrell was a dynamo who supervised the models, fashion show and advertising. She also ran an informal finishing school for Bullock's Wilshire employees, giving them an extra measure of social polish. When she left, it took three people to replace her.

Perhaps Farrell's greatest financial contribution to Bullock's Inc. was her remarkable skill as an advertising copy writer. One of Bullock's Wilshire's best retail weapons was "The Space," in-house slang for the back page of the second section of the Los Angeles Times. Store managers remember that page as the most productive advertising space in America. A dress advertised in a single ad could sell 500 to 600 units in three days. It was common to do $30,000 worth of business on one item shown in the ad, and sometimes the total reached $50,000, most of it at Bullock's Wilshire.

Every day, women across greater Los Angeles picked up the Times and went straight to that ad. What they found was an exquisitely sketched rendering of a garment, often imported, with every detail

— right down to the stitches. Bullock's Wilshire models regularly posed for the artists; photographs were never used.

Part of the appeal was Farrell's spry writing. A 1952 ad featuring women in tony millinery read: "Your new hat is small ... round ... and deep ... made of melusine ... the silky-soft felt that is this year's fashion sensation ... in the subtle shades of a Degas painting ... flattering and romantic ... from a collection ... millinery, second floor."

Another ad from the period for sportswear from the Playdeck beckoned melifluously: "Our velveteen failles ... the finely ribbed surface enhancing their bloom, their richness ... tailored to give a certain gallantry, a cavalier dash ..."

One of Farrell's best-remembered ads — and unusually risqué — said, "Spring is here ... let's all go out and get under a sailor." The headline ran over an elaborate drawing of a type of straw hat known as a "sailor." Always a lady, she swore that the double entendre was unintended.

The success of Bullock's Wilshire in its glory years is squarely laid on the vision of Winnett, a quirky expert at sensing what patrons wanted and delivering it. Both beloved and reviled, Winnett projected a commanding presence that reached every corner of the operation. Even his harshest critics quickly conceded that Winnett was one of the great merchant geniuses of the United States. For most of his life he was willing to experiment, to risk and to hold himself and others to the highest standards.

Among Winnett's many innovations was the highly successful introduction of a line of clothing especially for young women. He developed the concept in 1922, supposedly after hearing complaints from his daughters that they couldn't find suitable clothes. He opened the first "Collegienne" department that year, and devoted a whole floor to high school and college age young women when he built Bullock's Wilshire.

Winnett is also credited with developing what might now be known as resort wear or sportswear. Bullock's carriage trade clientele already had a taste for leisure, and Winnett catered to them with "play" clothes to take to the beach, lodge or polo grounds by encouraging vendors to create the garments.

He was an independent thinker, a quality he demonstrated early with his boyhood rejection of his given name, John William Jr., and his adoption of Percy Glen. Even his signature was bold, a fast line-jumping flourish underscored with a heavy line pointing diagonally upward on the page.

Winnett was extremely supportive of employees he favored, a practice he first learned from Arthur Letts, and created opportunities for them to succeed at the highest levels. He also had a prickly side to his personality that could emerge quickly and ruthlessly. Summary demotions and firings came along with field promotions and treats.

"If he liked you, he was wonderful. If he didn't like you, you might just as well quit," says long-time employee Dorothy Roth, a gift buyer who went to work at Bullock's Wilshire in 1943. Former store president Walter Bergquist calls Winnett both "brilliant" and "a tyrant" who kept many people needlessly on edge. Near the end of his life, in particular, Winnett became feared for his occasional spontaneous tirades that could reduce seasoned buyers to tears.

The diminutive — Winnett stood about five-feet-four — merchant was also mildly famous for being frequently surrounded with attractive young women, most of whom were Bullock's Wilshire models or other female employees.

He carried wrapped, hard candies in his pockets, handing the treats to women who pleased him while he made his rounds of the store. Winnett also sometimes carried a whistle, which he would toot at the models when they performed to his approval during the daily fashion shows.

"He loved the ladies," says a former employee, an assertion roundly supported by others who knew him. His enjoyment of female company was by no means a secret fancy. Groups of models were regular weekend guests at his large ranch in Walnut, and he took favorites on trips, especially to Hawaii.

Winnett once told a New York Times reporter about his management strategy: "Every day . . . I go around the store and I make it a point to shake hands with every one of the buyers. A man in this game has to know how to handle women. They like a pat on the back — anything but inattention."

Though Winnett often traveled from his downtown Bullock's store to Bullock's Wilshire in a chauffeur-driven Rolls Royce during the week, in later years he liked to drive his own huge, fin-tailed Cadillac convertible with the top down on weekend jaunts to Walnut. The large working ranch, once covering 1,800 acres, was called Rancho San Vicente, apparently after his in-town estate off San Vicente Drive near Santa Monica. Winnett Place, a cul de sac near the Riviera Country Club, marks the site where his estate was later sub-divided.

Winnett loved his country retreat, unwinding in a ranch house made of adobe with walls three feet thick. He could ride large horses and kept a few race horses for a time. Former guests describe him as a gracious host, and one remembers him wearing a barbecue apron with the names of models stitched across it. He would occasionally invite young men as well as young women to enjoy his weekend get-togethers — eating, swimming and relaxing.

But the Hawaii trips were legendary for their fun and the red carpet treatment the merchant received wherever he went there. Winnett loved the tropical resort and took first-class accommodations at the Royal Hawaiian hotel. Models who accompanied him were authorized to prepare for the trip by stocking up on Bullock's finest clothes, especially dresses, charged to his account. "We

Bullock's Wilshire's Christmas preparations were always spectacular.

Store models, shown here with Bullock's Wilshire president Walter Bergquist, created costumes from the store's famous ostrich-plumed Christmas tree, and performed a Folies Bergere in 1974.

Winnett's frequent trips to Hawaii were legendary for their fun and the red carpet treatment he received wherever he went.

could only buy chiffon," says Ivana Kislinger Mooney, "dresses that would float when we danced."

Dancing was a favorite pastime of Winnett's, and companions on his Hawaii trips were expected to join him for lunch, dinner and dancing each day. The evenings ended fairly early. "There was no hanky-panky or anything," says Mooney.

Winnett was a widower for all the years after his wife, Helen, died in 1949. They had two daughters, Glenn, who married Kenyon Boocock and moved to New York, and Kate, who married Walter Candy. Candy joined the Bullock's Wilshire staff as a merchandise manager in 1933.

Like John Bullock, Winnett was also active in community affairs, serving on various boards and commissions. Perhaps his most noteworthy civic achievement was the Citizens Transportation Committee, which he organized and directed. The committee made the first comprehensive study of a freeway system for Los Angeles, which it submitted to public officials in 1939. The study is credited with laying the foundation for today's freeways and expediting development.

Devoted to building on the retail customs that he and his partner had formulated, Winnett took over much of John Bullock's daily responsibilities in the later years. Despite his increasingly poor health, Bullock was in contact with store executives on a regular basis, and would speak with Winnett several times each day by telephone.

Winnett carefully maintained the rich history of traditions at Bullock's Wilshire, one of which was for many years the enormous Christmas tree, artfully constructed with white ostrich feathers for branches, that dominated the main foyer during the holidays. It was a crowd-pleaser that patrons adored, and they protested mightily if the tree didn't appear.

Freelance interior designer Mary Goodholme started in August supervising a laborious washing of the feathers by stock boys, who then had to blow on the ostrich plumes to dry and fluff them. Goodholme and her husband worked from closing time late into the night to ready the display. The spectacular tree, however beautiful, was prohibitively expensive, costing about $10,000 every three years for new white plumes.

Gradually the tree grew smaller in size as funds decreased, until it was sacrificed for a great party in 1974. Store models secretly readied costumes made from the feathers, then performed a Folies Bergere number for store president Bergquist, dancing and singing the favorite feathers out of Bullock's forever.

Another Bullock's Wilshire yule tradition catered specially to men who could afford the ultimate in pampered Christmas shopping. It was known as "Tower Five," for its location in John Bullock's sumptuous old office on the fifth floor.

The elite male patrons who shopped in Tower Five lived for a few hours like royalty on Cleopatra's barge. While the men sipped cocktails and grazed on hors d'oeuvres, Bullock's Wilshire models and other select female employees did their shopping for them. The women not only traveled throughout the store selecting possible gifts, but they would model them as well. As times changed, the tower tradition quietly disappeared.

Though the early years were majestic in many ways, they were not without their sorrows. Like his mentor Arthur Letts, Bullock struggled to keep his business thriving through some of the nation's worst economic times. Just weeks after Bullock's Wilshire opened its doors on September 29, 1929 the stock market crashed. The nation plunged into a depression that strained the resources of the men and their enterprise.

Four years later, John Bullock was dead. The public outpouring of grief and praise on the day of his death, Sept. 15, 1933, reflected his stature as a civic leader in burgeoning Los Angeles. His death was reported on the front page of the Los Angeles Times the next day, with a headline that read, "John G. Bullock's Rise to City Leadership Saga of Triumph for American Creed." The subhead was, "Merchant's Career Tale of Courageous Life."

Bullock had been warned by his doctor to slow down and delegate more of his responsibilities to younger managers, but Bullock felt under Depression-era conditions he had a duty to the public to stay on the job. After Bullock had suffered a series of what were believed to be minor heart attacks, he decided that he was forced to follow his physician's advice. Bullock left the cares of the store behind, and took his wife on a chauffeur-driven sight-seeing trip through San Francisco, the redwood forests and Yosemite Valley. Following his return to his home in Hancock Park, he succumbed to another heart attack. His wife was awakened to find her husband suffering from severe chest pains. She frantically called for the doctor, but before the physician could reach him, Bullock was dead. He was 62.

The complete responsibility for shepherding the Bullock's empire now rested on the shoulders of one man. Winnett received the news about his partner's unexpected death with great shock and sorrow. He immediately ordered the closing of the downtown store and Bullock's Wilshire. Memorial tributes were printed in the daily newspapers.

Bullock left behind his widow, Louise, and his two daughters, Mrs. Richard William Fewel and Miss Margaret S. Bullock.

Like the great Arthur Letts, Bullock had accepted the mantle of civic leader along with his great wealth. Perhaps his greatest contribution involved the four years he spent as a member of the board of directors of the Metropolitan Water District. As a passionate advocate of the Colorado River Aqueduct, he took a leading part in securing passage of the $220 million bond issue required to fund the project that brought badly needed water to Los Angeles in 1931.

Bullock also served at various times as a director of the YMCA, a trustee of Occidental College and president of the board of trustees of the Westlake

Presbyterian Church. The Retail Merchants Credit Association of Los Angeles elected him president 12 times. Bullock held memberships in the Los Angeles Athletic Club, the Los Angeles Country Club, the California Club and the Flintridge Country Club. Months prior to his death he was elected a member of the board of trustees of the California Institute of Technology.

Among the many plaudits for Bullock was one from a close friend, A.G. Arnold, of the Los Angeles Chamber of Commerce, who had this to say about the life of the distinguished merchant: "A man whose genius and rare ability have been well combined in the creation of a great commercial enterprise which has made renown through every corner of the nation by the comments of visitors to Los Angeles; a man, who, despite national and world-wide depression, continues the expansion and building of the enterprise and ideal; and lastly, a man who in spite of the intensive demands of that great business willingly turns his attention toward public service and accepts a role which carries with it not only work that is physically wearing, but tremendous responsibilities, as well."

But perhaps the most moving remembrance comes from the Minutes of a Special Meeting of the Board of Directors of Bullock's, Inc. on September 22, 1933:

"Our father in Heaven has called to His eternal home John Gillespie Bullock, the man we loved as our friend and followed as our leader.

"The life of John Gillespie Bullock was rugged. His personality was rich in its understanding of human nature. He was an apostle of Friendship, Sincerity and the Golden Rule, inflexible in his fidelity to every trust reposed in him. He was a pioneer upon the trail of progress, always thoughtful of his neighbors along the way.

"THEREFORE BE IT RESOLVED: That we shall carry on, and do our utmost to measure up to the standard of his ideals and expectations.

"To Mrs. Bullock, to his daughters Margaret and Helen, to his grandchildren — we pledge our devotion to the continuance of the great business that bears his name."

It was signed: - *P.G. Winnett, President*

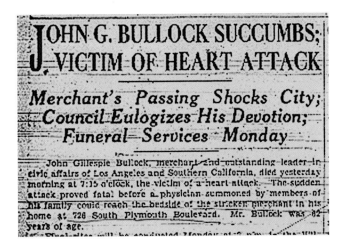

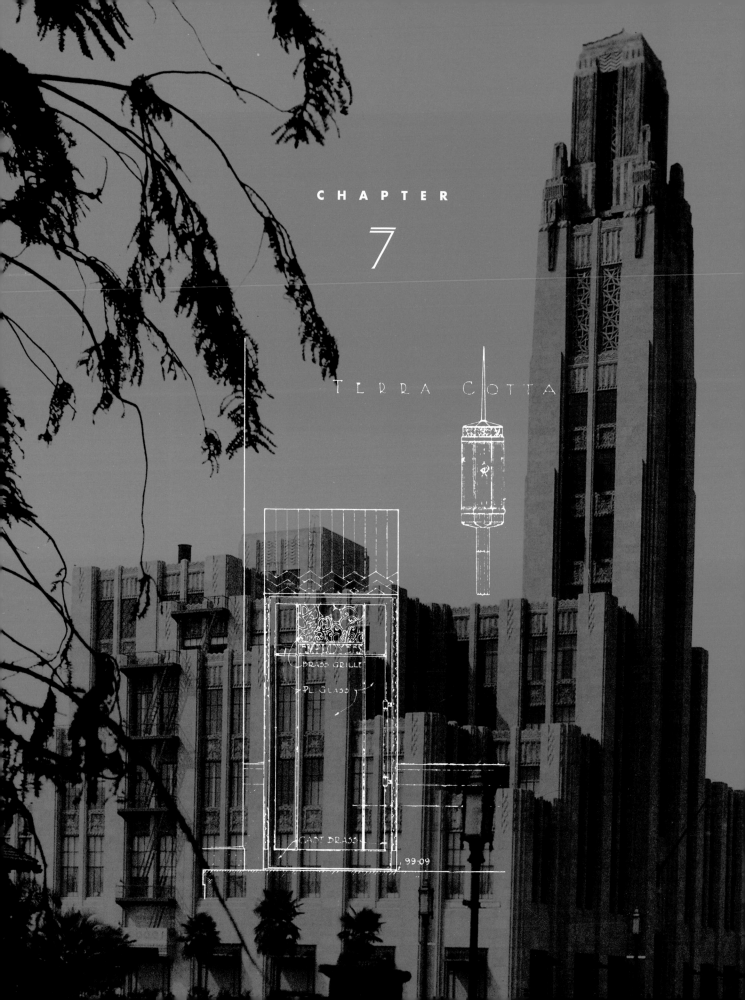

CHAPTER

7

TERRA COTTA

A BEAUTY FADES

*"Another venerable name in Southern
California retailing — Bullock's —
will soon disappear from the scene."*

— GEORGE WHITE,
LOS ANGELES TIMES, 1995

The keen business sense P. G. Winnett gleaned from the crisis years he spent with Arthur Letts and later John Bullock — coupled with his allegiance to Bullock's memory — carried the store through the last years of the Depression, and into the somber days of World War II, and enabled him to endure as a leading retailer.

Always tenacious and forward-thinking, Winnett made his most bold business decision in February 1944, when he spear-headed the merger of two of California's most famed retail houses: San Francisco's 68-year-old I. Magnin & Co., the purveyor of fine women's apparel, and 37-year-old Bullock's Inc. The result was a stunning business with 12 stores blanketing the West Coast with combined sales of $63 million.

By this time, Bullock's Inc. encompassed not only the original Seventh and Hill Street "Bullock's Downtown," with its 740,000-square-foot, six- building store, and "Bullock's Wilshire," but also included two suburban stores, "Bullock's Wilshire Palm Springs" and "Bullock's Pasadena."

Winnett's keen appreciation of the tastes of the carriage trade, and especially the retail tastes of women, made it easy for him to recognize Bullock's Inc. as the obvious choice for a white knight when the family-owned I. Magnin chain looked for a buyer in 1943. For years, I. Magnin's had remained the nation's second-largest retailer of top-priced women's wear, second only to New York's Saks Fifth Avenue. Bullock's had built an impeccable reputation and huge customer volume. The merger was a stroke of brilliance.

Mary Ann Magnin, the only American woman to ever head a mercantile empire, had founded the business with her own handmade line of children's and bridal clothes in 1876. She took an intense matriarchal interest in the business until her death in 1943 at age 95. Following her passing, two sons, John and Grover, who had been in the family business since the turn of the century, worked out the solid terms for a merger with Winnett. Now president of Bullock's Inc. and its principal stockholder at 30 percent, P. G. Winnett turned the ideal into merchandising fact.

No money exchanged hands. Stockholders of San Francisco-based I. Magnin received one Bullock's share in exchange for three and a half shares of I. Magnin. Grover headed the I. Magnin division until the end of 1950, the same year president P. G. Winnett became chairman of Bullock's-Magnin.

Winnett continued to rule the considerable holdings of Bullock's-Magnin in the next decade and his shrewdness in business matters became legendary. But Winnett's greatest battle was a 1964 proxy fight for control of the business, in which he was locked in combat against his own board of directors, a giant mercantile corporation and his son-in-law.

This time Winnett was alone in his struggle against the huge Federated Department Stores Inc. and his board, where he was the only vote against a proposed merger. Leading the charge for the dissident directors was Walter Candy, Winnett's son-in-law and his successor as president of Bullock's-Magnin.

The struggle was bitter and acrimonious. Winnett had built the empire and was the principal stockholder. Publicly he argued that his company had a better earnings record than Federated and a high book value. Worse, Winnett said, Bullock's famous unitization plan of empowering squads of buyers would probably be abandoned by the larger corporation.

Candy and his supporters pointed to the higher market price of Federated common stock. Shareholders would receive a bigger dividend even at the proposed 1.4-to-1 share exchange ratio.

Internally, Winnett had lost the confidence of his managers, who perceived a lack of desire on his part to expand the business and keep pace with the growing city. Market share was being lost at an alarming rate as competing department stores claimed new territories in the vast Southern California region. The vaunted unitization structure meant that opening a new branch was far more complex than just assembling bricks and mortar — whole teams of buyers had to be assembled and assimilated into the new market.

Winnett, key insiders felt, was too old at 83 to face the grind of building more stores. Further, his spontaneous tirades alarmed managers who began to question whether he could be counted on to behave rationally.

Publicly the coup was sold from a sheer business perspective. Candy and treasurer Mahlon E. Arnett, who had been with the company since 1929, campaigned in their proxy statements and in interviews with analysts and the press. Federated would offer the safety of geographical diversification and increased marketability of stock shares, they argued.

After four months of intramural combat, Winnett was deposed and Candy soon elected chairman of Bullock's-Magnin while Arnett became president. Bullock's and I. Magnin became separate operating divisions under the new ownership.

Winnett loyalists felt he had been unfairly dethroned.

"Walter Candy sold him out," says Winnett's friend Isabel Griffin. "Walter Candy was a nice man, a good-looking handsome man, but he was not a merchant. He married the boss's daughter."

Former Bullock's Wilshire general manager Richard Rifenbark calls it "a very logical decision" to go with Cincinnati, Ohio-based Federated. Walter Bergquist, former Bullock's Wilshire president who returned to manage Bullock's at the behest of Federated, says Candy had "seen the writing on the wall, and he'd been kicked

In Memoriam
P. G. WINNETT
of
BULLOCK'S
Distinguished Retailer
Beloved Friend

I. MAGNIN & CO

IN MEMORIAM

Mr P G Winnett

1881-1968

CO FOUNDER OF

BULLOCK'S

ALL BULLOCK'S STORES
WILL BE CLOSED
MONDAY, JULY 22
UNTIL 12 NOON

around long enough by Mr. Winnett. The son-in-law never had a free lunch being president of Bullock's."

Winnett's open interest in people and what they were doing and thinking had kept the merchant prince responsive to the changing modes of life and the resultant changes in a merchant's trade for many years. His allegiance was to the new and the original. Ironically, one of Winnett's favorite quotes was "Never fight change, it is our most valuable ally."

But the fight for control of ownership of the great enterprise took its human toll on the man, and Winnett was dead by July 1968. In honor of his fiftieth year in business, his board of directors and staff had presented him with an oil portrait of himself, painted by the eminent artist, Arthur Cahill. While Winnett acknowledged the gift with grace and pleasure, he declined to have it hung in his office at Bullock's Wilshire. "A man should not display his own portrait before the public eye," he said.

The portrait now hangs, quite fittingly, in the Winnett Center Building, which he endowed from his great retail fortune for student use at the California Institute of Technology.

Winnett did not live to see the greatest changes that took place within the empire he had built alongside Arthur Letts and John Bullock. During the merger-mad 1980s, the nation's biggest retail chains locked in a series of struggles that redefined the department store business. Decisions made in boardrooms and bankruptcy courts reeled Bullock's Inc. as the Southern California chain bobbed between giant corporations trying to create national empires and control the future of department store retailing.

While America's relentlessly efficient free-market system decided which retailing systems deserved to survive, the nature of the business evolved away from Bullock's narrow focus on neighborhood tastes to a more homogenized marketing formula that minimized costs at the expense of variety. One commentator likened the shift in retail methods to an evolution from a business of peacocks to one of velociraptors.

Bullock's Wilshire's reign as the fairest peacock in Los Angeles had been a struggle since the city's post World War II boom created many new, more distant suburbs that slowly began to draw the commercial life force out of the Mid-Wilshire district. The store countered with special events, many of them lavish black-tie affairs that brought together foreign dignitaries and the cream of society. But the combined forces of urban decay and changing retail standards would eventually grind Bullock's Wilshire under.

Bergquist's successor, Jerome Nemiro, who served as president from 1974 until the chain changed hands in the late 1980s, fought long and hard to keep Bullock's Wilshire special. It was on his watch that a separate group was created within Bullock's to uphold the mystique of the Wilshire Boulevard store. The group was called Bullocks Wilshire, without an apostrophe in Bullocks, eventually consisting of six stores in addition to the namesake. They were located in Palos Verdes, Newport Beach, Woodland Hills, Palm Springs, La Jolla and Palm Desert. Mail order sales were so successful it was almost like having an eighth branch.

"When I first got [to Bullock's Wilshire], the community thought we were just another Bullock's store. I felt that if we had a future, we had to be different," says Nemiro.

The merchandise and advertising were of a more exclusive level, delivered with the same kind of rapt attention to style and personal service that Bullock and Winnett believed in.

"We catered to a more mature, sophisticated audience," says Nemiro, who still holds a reverent respect for the professionalism and devotion of his buyers.

Ultimately the dedication of the staff wasn't enough to fight the changes going on in the retail industry.

Designated a historical landmark, Bullock's Wilshire is listed in the National Register of Historic Places and was declared Los Angeles Historic Cultural Monument No. 56 in 1969. It is considered an Art Deco masterpiece.

THE NEW YORK TIMES, SUNDAY, JULY 5, 1964.

Personality: Retailers in Hot Proxy Fight

Federated's Lazarus Stakes Company's Prestige on Deal

By LEONARD SLOANE

At the special meeting of stockholders of Federated Department Stores, Inc., scheduled for Cincinnati on July 17, Ralph Lazarus, president, will be some 2,200 miles away in Los Angeles.

Mr. Lazarus will be there anxiously awaiting the results of another special meeting of stockholders of Bullock's, Inc., the big West Coast retail chain. At both meetings, stockholders will vote on the proposal to merge Bullock's into Federated and thereby create a coast-to-coast retailing organization with annual sales of more than $1 billion.

"But I don't expect to attend the Bullock's meeting,"

Ralph Lazarus

and established a men's cloth-

Winnett of Bullock's Is Only Director to Oppose Merger

By GLADWIN HILL

Special to The New York Times

Los Angeles.

P. G. Winnett, spearheading one of the hottest proxy fights on the business scene, isn't letting it interfere with his habitual close scrutiny of the daily operations of Bullock's, Inc., the $100 million department store organization that he heads.

"Every day I have lunch at a different store," the silvery-haired chairman says. "I go around the store, and I make it a point to shake hands with every one of the buyers. A man in this game has to know how to handle women. They like a pat on the back—anything but inat-

P. G. Winnett

phens, ruled that 110,416

All 21 Bullock's to Be Converted to Macy's Stores

By GEORGE WHITE
TIMES STAFF WRITER

Another venerable name in Southern California retailing—Bullock's—will soon disappear from the scene.

Federated Department Stores confirmed Thursday that it will convert its 21-store Bullock's chain into Macy's stores to place its statewide merchandising operations under one retailing roof.

Although the change will erase the Bullock's marquee 88 years after the first Bullock's department store opened at 7th Street and Broadway in Los Angeles, it will introduce the famed Macy's name to Southern California for the first time.

Federated executives disclosed their plans to The Times one day after the company completed its acquisition of Los Angeles-based

Corporate manuerving finally reached a peak in February 1988 when New York-based R.H. Macy & Co. offered $6.1 billion to take over Federated Department Stores. This prompted a bidding war with Campeau Corp. of Canada, which had launched an earlier takeover bid for Federated.

A compromise was reached in April 1988 whereby Campeau won control of Federated in a $6.6 billion deal that allowed Macy to buy Federated's Bullock's and I. Magnin divisions for $1.1 billion. It was a costly win for Macy, which continued to lose money as sales plummeted during a nationwide recession. Nearly depleted of cash, Macy filed for Chapter 11 bankruptcy protection in January 1992.

In 1995 Federated resurfaced, announcing that it had purchased half of Macy's debt. Federated officers also spoke of their desire to possibly merge with Macy.

Macy initially resisted the merger but eventually it was accepted by the board. In a matter of weeks Macy and Federated went from being the Hatfields and McCoys to being the Romeo and Juliet of retailing. While Wall Street enthusiastically embraced the marriage, some consumer advocates feared shoppers would have to pay for the acquisition with higher prices. Bullock's and other department stores caught up in the buy-out frenzy already had been under tremendous pressure to help corporate owners pay interest on their debts.

Wall Street's opinion was that the merger would create a national retailing powerhouse that would benefit from the consolidation of management and support operations, as well as the elimination of overlapping, underperforming stores.

The corporate culture had changed. Macy shifted its buying operations from Los Angeles to Atlanta, a move that would have been inconceivable to John Bullock and P.G. Winnett. Analysts said Bullock's was losing touch with its upscale customers. As part of the consolidation Macy converted all of the Bullocks Wilshire stores — the elite division within the Bullock's chain — to I. Magnins in 1990.

By the time Federated regained control in 1992, the I. Magnin store at Bullock's Wilshire was being torn from several directions. Although the national economy was in recovery, Southern California continued to grapple with the worst recession since the Great Depression. The mid-city stretch of Wilshire Boulevard that had once been considered "uptown" and a highly prestigious address had been falling out of favor for some time. Businesses that had made Mid-Wilshire home for many years had been relocating their offices to newer buildings in other parts of the city. The aging housing stock around Bullock's Wilshire became less and less likely to be a source of customers, and patrons from outlying areas were offered more and more alternatives closer to home.

Crime and, more devastatingly, the fear of it made many patrons leery of visiting Bullock's Wilshire. Their worst fears became Bullock's nightmare in July 1992, when riots erupted in Los Angeles following the acquittal of four city policemen accused of beating motorist Rodney King. Bullock's Wilshire was a tempting target for looters, who devastated the first floor.

"We closed the store at three in the afternoon, and by four they were in the building," remembers Roy Robbins, who was general manager at the time. Thieves showed indiscriminate tastes, he says, such as using a piece of Lalique crystal valued at $3,000 to smash a glass counter and steal a lipstick. Every display case was broken on the first floor, but the damage was confined there. The elevators had been stopped before the employees left, and looters either didn't know where the stairs were or didn't choose to use them.

Perhaps the most searing image of the 1992 riots was a skyline filled with scores of burning buildings. Bullock's Wilshire easily could have been among them because the store's attackers attempted to set at least three fires.

Fortunately none of them took hold and the store's historical treasures remained intact despite the financial ruin. A newspaper account valued the loss at $10 million, while Robbins puts it closer to $15 million.

The store reopened within a week, but business never fully recovered and the neighborhood continued to falter. The nearby Sheraton-Town House hotel, which had begun operations the same year as Bullock's Wilshire, closed its doors in February 1993. Another nearby once-glamorous hotel, The Ambassador, had been shuttered since 1989. On top of everything else, construction of Metro Rail, a subway running under Wilshire Boulevard, disrupted traffic along the street.

The end came in March 1993 when R.H. Macy & Co. announced it would close 11 stores nationwide. Among them was the struggling Wilshire Boulevard branch.

Though P.G. Winnett's choice for location for his suburban expansion had proven to be no folly, he surely would have found irony in one of the reasons it had finally failed: in the beginning, founders weren't certain patrons would drive that far out of town to shop. In the end, patrons wouldn't drive that far into town.

RENOVATION AND RESURRECTION

The exquisite alliance between art and commerce envisioned by John Bullock ended when the doors of Bullock's Wilshire closed in April 1993.

Generations of loyal patrons mourned the loss of a cherished friend and architectural preservationists were incensed to see another of their city's great, signature buildings threatened with destruction. Passionate public appeals and legal wrangling followed, yet the future of the beloved cultural icon remained uncertain.

The once regal "monument to modernism" was now a fragile touchstone to the past, susceptible to artistic defacement and structural ruin. Admirers of the Art Deco masterpiece feared that the prized building would limp on as some unglamorous enterprise, or even worse, fall victim to demolition.

"The once dignified store [now] has the air about it dreaded by city officials and preservationists," wrote the Los Angeles Times. "It feels like a swap meet. Boxes of old Christmas decorations clutter what used to be the Menswear room. Messy piles of draperies and banners cover the floor of a former salon for crystal. Hundreds of dusty chairs and crowds of naked mannequins fill dress departments. Everything has a price tag on it."

Above:
Southwestern's Library, circa
1933.

Left:
An early student banquet at
Southwestern University School
of Law, circa 1920's.

Bullock's Wilshire's closing was attributed to its unfashionable location and the financial troubles of its new owner, R.H. Macy & Co., who had filed for bankruptcy protection in 1992. Public dismay at the closure worsened after it was learned that some of the store's prized fixtures had been removed and relocated to other I. Magnin and Bullock's stores in California.

Los Angeles Mayor Richard Riordan and tenacious preservationists urged that Macy's return dozens of chandeliers, sconces, and antique furniture pieces that had been taken away. In a December 1993 letter to Macy's Chairman Myron Ullman III, Riordan wrote that the building was "one of the most significant historic-cultural monuments in the city of Los Angeles." Riordan emphasized that Bullock's Wilshire should "remain intact as an anchor of the Wilshire corridor."

City officials did not want the missing fixtures forgotten in Macy's ongoing bankruptcy hearings. Bullock's Wilshire had been designated as a Los Angeles historic and cultural monument and was included in the National Register of Historic Places, but federal and municipal laws protected only the building and not the moveable fixtures. Undeterred, the Los Angeles Conservancy vigorously lobbied for return of the artistic treasures based on their importance to Los Angeles' cultural history.

After a year of delicate negotiations, Macy's agreed to return all of the historically significant fixtures and furnishings it had removed. Macy's decision was thought to be the first major return of historic fixtures by a property owner who was not required to do so and the move was applauded by city leaders and preservationists. Nearly every piece, including crystal chandeliers, furniture, clocks, urns, and other bits of Bullock's precious legacy came back.

Although intact, the store now found itself about to join a growing list of disappearing Los Angeles landmarks. It seemed almost certain that Bullock's Wilshire would fall victim to the same conditions that had forced the closure of other mid-Wilshire institutions such as the Ambassador Hotel, the historic Sheraton Town House, nearby Brown Derby restaurant and Perino's.

Speculation continued to rage over the building's fate, and there seemed few viable alternatives for proper use of the structure. Some argued that the building should be converted to an art museum, others wanted the structure to remain an upscale retail establishment, others lobbied for the regal dowager to be retrofitted as commercial office space. Retail uses of the structure as a specialty store were severely restricted because of Bullock's Wilshire's design. John Bullock had intended that clothing be shown to his patrons in a unique setting with live models. There were all sorts of practical problems: there was little space for clothing racks, there were no escalators to accommodate large numbers of shoppers, and any use of shopping carts was impractical.

The dubious future of the prized building took a refreshing turn in May 1993 when Dean Leigh Taylor of nearby Southwestern University School of Law approached then Mayor Tom Bradley about the possibility of acquiring the Bullock's Wilshire building and two lots adjacent to the Bullock's property as well as Macy's 39-year ground lease with the California Institute of Technology. (Caltech was the owner of the land upon which the building was located). Situated across the street at 675 South Westmoreland Ave., Southwestern now viewed the stately building as a possible addition to the thriving but cramped law school. Mayor Bradley, an alumnus of the law school, was enthusiastic about the proposal and helped bring together Taylor and the chief executive officer at R.H. Macy & Co. in New York to begin negotiations.

Taylor made it clear that should the school acquire Bullocks' Wilshire, it would also accept the obligations of stewardship that the occupant of such an historic structure was expected to sustain. Southwestern was committed to attaining the highest level of adaptive reuse and rigorous restoration to ensure that the cultural and historic areas of the building would remain intact.

A negotiating team was soon dispatched by Taylor to represent Southwestern, but to the dismay of supporters, by summer the deal had fallen apart. The concerns of various preservation groups added to the complex issues and emotions at stake, and in part complicated resolution of the impending sale. It wasn't until October 1993 that Taylor executed a letter of intent with Macy's to develop a purchase agreement for the building subject to bankruptcy court approval.

Passions regarding the building's fate continued to escalate. Hoping that a bargain could be struck between all parties that would preserve the building and serve the interests of the law school, Taylor never set foot inside Bullock's Wilshire during the stressful negotiation period in a wishful gesture of good luck. Despite the letter of intent, Taylor still faced the process of open bidding in New York City in federal bankruptcy court. Southwestern's toughest competition for acquisition of the historic structure was an electronics store that had met the qualifications to enter into open bidding as a legitimate purchaser. Wearing his best poker face, Taylor watched as the bidding for the architectural gem rose higher.

The winning bid in the judicial auction ultimately went to Southwestern at a price of $4.8 million. Environmental mediation and additional closing details were negotiated and, by July, Taylor commenced talks with Caltech concerning purchase of the ground beneath the structure. A final deal was concluded in three eventful weeks.

In addition to the $4.8 million purchase price and additional payments to Caltech of $3.8 million for purchase of the land, Southwestern pledged to spend an additional $9.5 million for restoration of the building's core structure and various other upgrades. Southwestern anticipated that the school's total renovation would ultimately exceed $20 million.

The first phase of the school's renovation program involved transfer of the school's 365,000-volume library to floors one and two of Bullock's Wilshire under the watchful eyes of Professor Linda Whisman, Director of Southwestern's Law Library. Students now study in reading rooms on the ground floor amid the art trea-

sures that dazzled patrons of the store for 63 years. By the turn of the century, the building will be fully converted to school use, with other academic program needs and administrative offices accommodated.

The main entrance to the building remains as originally designed, and students and library patrons enter the structure via the legendary porte cochere. The former Perfume Hall still glows from the walls and ceilings of rose-colored St. Genevieve marble but now greets visitors as an elegant entry area.

The library's reference room west of the Perfume Hall, where the Sportswear department once stood still boasts the stunning abstract mural by artist Gjura Stojano. Library shelving at counter height facilitates the use of indexes and reference materials and allows full view of the historic decorative features of the room.

On the south side of the first floor, a wide corridor with original travertine flooring leads to the new elevator and internal staircase. Nearby, stacks house the law school's extensive collection of federal practice and research materials. The former Palm Court still features distinctive bronze-colored metal palm trees but now marks the entrance to the school's state-of-the-art computer lab, casual reading room, video room and California collection. Specially designed study carrels which evoke the structure's Art Deco themes will be cabled for network access by students with laptop computers.

The former Menswear department, designed by Jock Peters and reminiscent of Frank Lloyd Wright's concrete block houses features the California law collection. Wall and ceiling ornamentation remains unchanged, with new wood bookcases replacing clothing display racks.

The legendary Irene's Salon, located on the second floor, slightly modified, accommodates a clear aisle to the main stack area which houses the legal treatise collection. Study carrels along the exterior walls take advantage of the 14-foot-high windows.

The foreign, international and comparative law collection brings a serious note to the highly feminine

*The "Spirit of Sports" remains
exuberantly over studious new
patrons.*

former Lingerie department. The walls and columns of this room are faced with pink glass and ornamented with gold, silver and mirror inlays. The metal end panels for the shelving in this area reflect the character of the black tubular steel furnishings which originally accented the room. The basement, the only portion of the building remodeled, houses computer learning centers, out-of-state law collections, legal periodicals and a legal research classroom.

While keeping in the aesthetic spirit of the cultural landmark, the library provides state of the art functionality in a setting with a style and character that would be impossible to recreate today.

Restoration architect Ronald A. Altoon, FAIA, grew up in the Los Feliz district of Los Angeles and shopped often with family members at Bullock's Wilshire and has great affection for the edifice. "I've hung on to many a purse walking through there. It's so unlike any other building. Though the spaces were grand, they were actually a mixture of formal and informal."

As an architect he was also smitten with the remarkable synergy generated by the teams that worked together so many years ago. "When you look at the plans drawn in those days and realize what an enormous gap there is between the suggestions on those drawings and the realized craft, you can tell it must have been an extraordinary relationship between architects and artisans to create that in the field. It's really quite overwhelming."

The architectural firm of Altoon + Porter had already been retained by Southwestern in anticipation of a new campus addition before Bullock's Wilshire's closure was announced. As the Parkinsons had to scrap early plans for the store after visiting the Paris exposition, so did Altoon set aside his plans for an on-site expansion of the law school after the Bullock's acquisition was finalized.

"I was ecstatic," Altoon said of getting the opportunity to work with Bullock's Wilshire. Fortunately his firm had substantial experience renovating historical properties throughout the world. A highly praised effort close to home was the successful conversion of an old

Restoration architect Ronald A. Altoon, FAIA.

fire station in downtown Los Angeles to Engine Co. No. 28 restaurant.

In one key respect, Bullock's Wilshire lent itself adroitly to its new application — both a library and a department store from the Bullock's era are designed to accommodate only the highest reach of the average human hand, with decoration placed above that point. Thus the scales of their uses are very compatible. The art works that hovered engagingly over the sales floor are easily visible over the bookshelves.

Further, the law library has not been designed to maximize available footage, but to showcase the artistic environment. Dramatic spaces such as the Saddle Shop and Irene's Salon are preserved as reading rooms. Study tables and carrels have been designed to conceal all wiring and computer links. A new stairway and elevator have been added but carefully concealed behind the once-public spaces of Bullock's Wilshire. The former Playdeck mezzanine is now library administration offices. The third, fourth and fifth floors are intended to serve as future classrooms and administrative offices.

Altoon assigned two special teams within his firm to take different viewpoints during the design process — one was acting as an advocate for the building and one was looking out for the tenant. Comment from local preservationists and the city's Cultural Heritage Commision was also solicited. In most cases preference was given to maintaining or recreating the special features designed in 1929.

The architect remains deeply impressed with the icon of another era saying, "I think John Parkinson and his son are architects who left us an incredible legacy, not only in this building but all the others they designed in this city. Each was a seminal piece of style, so our work was also a commitment to maintain their legacy here."

Bullock's Wilshire may be the most preeminent building of historical value in Los Angeles, Altoon says. "It's an extraordinary thing that an architect comes upon a shell like this that is so carefully considered, that is such a part of our cultural history as well as our architectural history that's been part of the life of this city for so many generations.

"To have the opportunity to breath new life into that building in an institutional way, in a way that carries that legacy forward, is really a wonderful challenge," says the architect.

Southwestern, a well established, highly regarded institution, has been an important part of the Los Angeles legal community since 1911. Notable graduates in addition to Mayor Bradley include California Supreme Court Justice Stanley Mosk, U.S. Representative Julian Dixon, California Treasurer Matt Fong and Los Angeles County prosecutor Marcia Clark.

Mayor Bradley applauded the school's efforts, "Southwestern University School of Law achieved the acquisition of the century when it acquired the Bullock's Wilshire building. The Bullock's building is not only a cultural icon in the heart of Los Angeles, but represents an historical turning point in retailing industry in Los Angeles and its history will be preserved and retold over and over again through its preservation."

Justice Arleigh Woods, an alumna of Southwestern and chair of its board of trustees, was pleased with the school's acquisition of the historic structure. "It is so exciting to realize that this exquisite architectural jewel is now the face of Southwestern University School of Law. This represents an investment in the viability of the inner city and the beauty of Los Angeles."

Dean Taylor was ecstatic over the acquisition saying, "It was extremely fortuitous for us that the Bullock's

Dean Leigh H. Taylor.

Wilshire building became available when it did. Southwestern was beginning to burst at the seams, particularly in the Law Library, and we needed to expand our facilities to accommodate growth in terms of the collection as well as for future academic needs.

"This project enables us to assemble one of the most extraordinary, inspiring law school settings in the country, and at the same time to preserve a treasured historic cultural monument."

It wasn't easy. On a number of occasions school administrators were reminded that it would have been infinitely less difficult to build a brand new structure.

Pride and a profound sense of reverence for Bullock's Wilshire have guided all the efforts to preserve the building and prolong its life in what Altoon called a "politely respectful use," likening the law school to a hermit crab attaching itself to a magnificent shell and moving forward.

"I am happy that the law school has taken over the building because I can't think of a better use for it than the library of another prestigious institution," said former Bullock's Wilshire president Jerome Nemiro. "From my experience I know they will treat the building with respect and consideration."

The refurbishment of Bullock's Wilshire is considered one of the most extensive Art Deco renovations undertaken in this decade. According to Mitzi March Mogul, president of the Art Deco Society of Los Angeles, the three most significant restorations of Art

Bullock's Wilshire was more than a department store, it was a state of mind for many of its patrons. One architectural critic in 1929 described the store as "a trip abroad, a gracious lesson in architecture, a complete course in decorative art, and altogether a magnificent gesture."

Deco buildings world-wide include the Wiltern Theater of Los Angeles, Bullock's Wilshire, and the Savoy Theater in London.

"Bullock's Wilshire is such a significant building," Mogul says, "any restoration must proceed carefully. The only other adaptive restoration comparable to Bullock's Wilshire in terms of importance and magnitude is the Wiltern Theater located nearby on Wilshire Blvd."

Through the acquisition of Bullock's Wilshire, Southwestern has achieved the enviable opportunity to create an extraordinary campus setting. But the school faces enormous difficulties associated with such stewardship, a formidable task that will receive intense scrutiny.

Bullock's Wilshire will begin its new life as a cathedral of learning 67 years after John Bullock first opened the store's massive bronze doors in 1929. The cathedral of commerce that Bullock presented to the city he adored captured the hearts and imagination of the people of Los Angeles. Under the guardianship of its new owners, and the watchful eyes of preservationists, it will endure in its new role in the social and cultural life of the city.

Taylor points out, "When John Bullock and his colleagues built this landmark, I'm sure they had no idea it would ever be anything other than a specialty store. They must have known, however, that it would always remain one of the architectural anchors of the city. And now in this new era of the Information Age, what could be more befitting this magnificent building then a center of information, one of the finest law library collections you will find anywhere.

"At Southwestern we are extremely proud to be the stewards of this important piece of cultural heritage, and we will continue to ensure that it is preserved and respected for generations to come."

BIBLIOGRAPHY

INTERVIEWS

Ronald A. Altoon, Ursula Frei Banning, Walter Bergquist, David Gebhard, Kenny Farrow, Scott Field, Isabel Griffin, Kiyo Hirayama, Gary Kurutz, Angela Lansbury, Debra Leathers, Leigh Taylor, Albert C. Martin, Sheila McMillan, Peg Meehan, Mitzi March Mogul, Ivana Mooney, Jerome Nemiro, Richard Rifenbark, Roy Robbins, Dorothy Roth, Peggy Smith, Marty Trent, Sylvia Wallis, Martin Ely Weil, and Shirley Wilson.

LIBRARIES AND COLLECTIONS

Los Angeles Central Library, Los Angeles
California State Archives, Sacramento
Los Angeles City Archives, Los Angeles
University Research Library, University of California Los Angeles
Mott/Merge Collection, Sacramento
Hearst Collection, Los Angeles
Security Pacific Collection, Los Angeles
Jock Peters Collection, Library of History, Art and Architecture, University of California, Santa Barbara
Edward L. Doheny Jr. Library, University of Southern California
Architecture and Fine Arts Library, University of Southern California

BOOKS

Birmingham, Nan Tillison. *Store*. New York: G.P. Putnam's and Sons. 1978.

Chandler, Raymond. *The Big Sleep*. New York: Vintage Books. 1988.

Davis, Margaret Leslie. *Rivers in the Desert: William Mulholland and the Inventing of Los Angeles*. New York: HarperCollins 1993.

Hancock, Ralph. *Fabulous Boulevard*. New York: Funk & Wagnalls Company, 1949.

Hendrickson, Robert. *The Grand Emporiums: The Illustrated History of America's Great Department Stores*. New York: Stein and Day, 1979.

Gebhard, David and Von Breton, Harriet. *Los Angeles in the Thirties*. Los Angeles: Hennessey and Ingnalls, 1989.

Katz, Ephraim. *The Film Encyclopedia*. New York: HarperCollins. 1994.

Hay, Peter. *MGM: When the Lion Roars*. Atlanta: Turner Publishing Inc. 1991.

Kilner, William H.B. *Arthur Letts 1862-1923*. Los Angeles: Young & McCallister, 1927.

Mahoney, Tom. *The Great Merchants: America's Foremost Retail Institutions and the People Who Made Them Great*. New York: Harper and Row, 1966.

McWilliams, Carey. *Southern California Country: An Island on the Land*. New York: Drell, Sloan & Pierce, 1946.

Parker, Robert Mile. *Los Angeles*. New York; Harcourt. 1984.

Parkinson Centennial; 1884-1994. Los Angeles: Parkinson Field Associates, 1994.

Riva, Maria. *Marlene Dietrich*. New York: Alfred A. Knopf. 1993.

Starr, Kevin. *Material Dreams: Southern California Through the 1920s*. New York: Oxford Press, 1990.

Starr, Kevin. *Inventing the Dream, California Through the Progressive Era*. New York: Oxford University Press, 1985.

Ward, Elizabeth. *Raymond Chandler's Los Angeles*. New York: The Overlook Press, 1987.

SIGNED ARTICLES

Bristol, Edith, "John G. Bullock Tells Why It Pays To Spend Millions for Art in Business," Western Advertising and Western Business, Feb. 6, 1930, pp. 60-62.

Flint, Ralph. "Jock Peters, Creative Art," September 1932, pp. 31- 32.

Allen, Harris. "A Building Designed for Today, An Expression of Contemporary Ideas Deserving Consideration," California Arts & Architecture. January, 1930, pp. 53-55.

Lloyd, R.E. "What We Learned From the Bullock Job," Electrical West, Vol. 67, No. 5, pp. 218-220.

Newman, Morris. "Past to the Future: Historic Architecture Firm Takes New Office on Spring Street Site of Former Glories," Los Angeles Downtown News, Vol. 21, No. 45, Nov. 9, 1992.

Peters, Jock. "What's Behind This Modernism Anyway?" The Mohawk Rug Retailer. Vol. iii, No. 1, Sept.- Oct. 1928, pp. 2-4.

Schindler, Pauline G. "A Significant Contribution to Culture: The Interior of a Great California Store As An Interpretation of Modern Life," California Arts & Architecture. January 1930, pp. 23-25.

Kurutz, Gary. "A Contemporary Cathedral of Commerce: Bullock's Wilshire As Documented by the Mott Studios," California State Library Foundation Bulletin. No. 50, January 1995, pp. 15-23.

UNSIGNED ARTICLES

"A Store for the Motorized Carriage Trade." Architectural Forum. May 1948.

"Bullock's Wilshire Boulevard Store - Los Angeles." The Architect and Engineer. December 1929. pp. 45-50.

"Bullock's Wilshire Department Store Los Angeles." Architectural Record, LXVIII. January 1930, pp. 51-64

"Building Prospects for 1929 Are Equally as Good as Those Reported a Year Ago," Southwest Builder and Contractor. Jan. 4, 1929, pp. 41-42.

"Fact Sheets on Historic-Cultural Monuments," Cultural Heritage Board Municipal Art Dept. of Los Angeles, Aug. 6, 1962- June 6, 1973, #56.

"Southwestern Acquires Landmark." Southwestern University School of Law Bulletin, Vol. 83 No. 2, Bulletin, Spring, 1994, pp. 5-12.

Program, Funeral Services of Mr. P.G. Winnett, Church of the Recessional, Forest Lawn. July 22, 1968.

"The Bullock Way," The Bullock's Organization, September 1933.

NEWSPAPERS

Illustrated Daily News
Los Angeles Evening Herald
Los Angeles Record
Los Angeles Examiner
Los Angeles Evening Express
Los Angeles Times
Los Angeles Herald-Examiner

On-Line Research Courtesy of West Publishing Company

ACKNOWLEDGMENTS

I have loved Bullock's Wilshire since the first day I stepped inside the store as a six-year-old child. I would like to thank the following people for allowing me the opportunity to write about this Art Deco treasure that has become indelibly etched into Los Angeles' cultural soul.

I am grateful to Dorothy Molstad, West Publishing Co., for access to Westlaw and other research materials.

Special thanks to Ronald A. Altoon, Walter Bergquist, Ed Brown, Karen Chappelle, Mona Danford, Carol Easton, Robert Feinberg, Noel Riley Fitch, Jeffrey Forer, Scott Field, Candace Gates, David Gebhard, Jane Gilman, Keri McKenzie Kemble, Jayne Kistner, Gary Kurutz, Angela Lansbury, Debra Leathers, Keith Lehrer, Albert C. Martin, Dr. Brian Young McLean, Stephen Mitchell, Ivana Kislinger Mooney, Mitzi March Mogul, Albert and Loretta Morgenstern, Jerome Nemiro, Jean Penn, Pam Post, Richard Rifenbark, Roy Robbins, Peter Shamray, Leslie Steinberg, Leigh Taylor, Chris Turner, Amelia Vetrone, Katherine Wallace, Sylvia Wallis, Thomas Waller, Linda A. Whisman, and Shirley Wilson.

A very special thanks to T. Sumner Robinson and Jim Bellows.

I am especially indebted to Ann Gray of Balcony Press and my literary agent, Richard Curtis.

— *Margaret Leslie Davis*
Windsor Square, 1996

MARGARET LESLIE DAVIS' book *Rivers in the Desert: William Mulholland and the Inventing of Los Angeles* (HarperCollins) was the first major biography of the genius engineer who built the Los Angeles Aqueduct, and was the winner of the Golden Spur Award for Best Non-Fiction Book by the Western Writers of America. Davis, an alumna of Georgetown University and Southwestern University School of Law, writes a monthly column, "Courtroom Classics," for the Los Angeles Daily Journal. She is Arts and Humanities editor for "excite," a new media web navigation service based in Mountain View, California (http://www.excite.com). She is currently writing the biography of oil baron Edward L. Doheny.

ROGER VINCENT conducted interviews for this book and contributed as a writer. He is editor of the California Real Estate Journal, a monthly news magazine serving the commercial real estate industry. Vincent has been a fixture on the real estate scene for 12 years, having served as real estate editor of the Los Angeles Business Journal before founding the Real Estate Journal in 1988. He is the former executive editor of Davis Newspaper Group.

In memory of David Gebhard, educator, preservationist, architect.
1928–1996

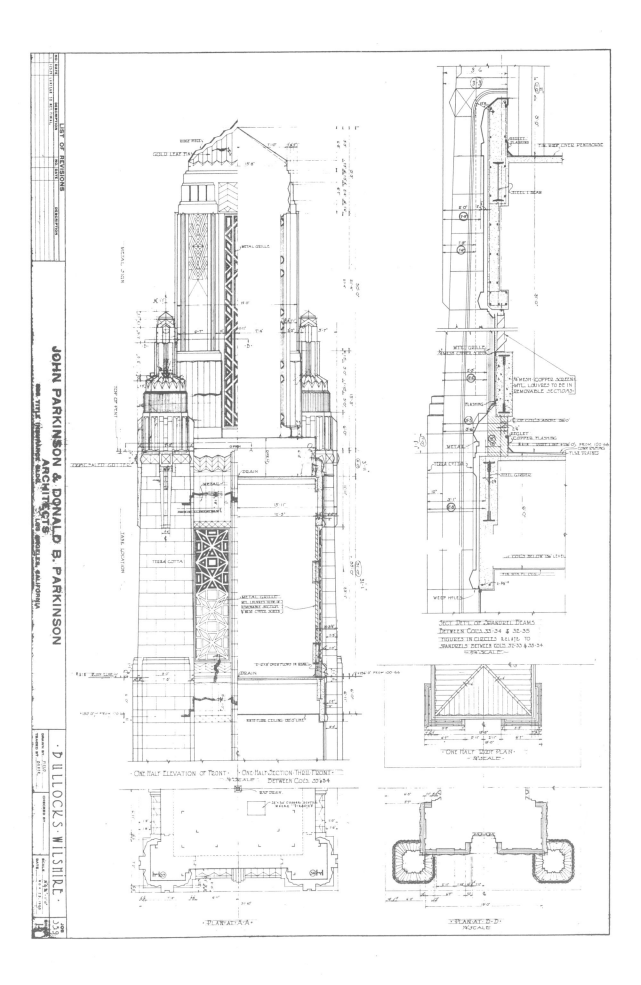

JOHN PARKINSON & DONALD B. PARKINSON

ARCHITECTS

LOS ANGELES, CALIFORNIA

LIST OF REVISIONS

BULLOCKS WILSHIRE

·ONE·HALF·ELEVATION·OF·FRONT· ·ONE·HALF·SECTION·THRU·FRONT·
BETWEEN·COLS·33&34

·PLAN·AT·A·A·

SECT·DETL·OF·SPANDREL·BEAMS·
BETWEEN·COLS·33-34 & 32-35
FIGURES·IN·CIRCLES·RELATE·TO·
SPANDRELS·BETWEEN·COLS·32-33 & 33-34

·ONE·HALF·ROOF·PLAN·

·PLAN·AT·D·D·